ALGEBRA I

Homework Helper

© 2006 Carnegie Learning, Inc.

Carnegie Learning™

THE COGNITIVE TUTOR® COMPANY

Carnegie Learning™
THE COGNITIVE TUTOR® COMPANY

Pittsburgh, PA
Phone 888.851.7094
Fax 412.690.2444

www.carnegielearning.com

Acknowledgements

We would like to thank those listed below who helped to prepare the Cognitive Tutor® *Algebra I* Homework Helper.

Michael and Emily Amick
Autumn Morin
Michele Covatto
The Carnegie Learning Development Team

ISBN 1-932409-62-9
Homework Helper

Printed in the United States of America
1-2006-VH
2-2006-VH
3-2006-VH
4-2006-VH

Introduction

Welcome to Carnegie Learning's Cognitive Tutor® *Algebra I* curriculum!
We are excited that your student will be part of our unique approach to learning mathematics.

A Better Approach to Mathematics for Your Student

Research and field tests have validated that the Carnegie Learning's approach helps students to improve their course grades and overall achievement. Whether your student excels or struggles with mathematics, the Cognitive Tutor *Algebra I* curriculum will help your student strengthen skills, content knowledge, and confidence.

The curriculum uses a scientifically-researched approach based on 20 years of investigation into how students think, learn, and apply new knowledge in mathematics. Based on extensive research and design at Carnegie Mellon University and field-tested by leading mathematics educators, our approach uses students' intuitive problem solving abilities as a powerful bridge to a more formal understanding of mathematics.

Software and Textbook Blended Curriculum

The Cognitive Tutor *Algebra I* curriculum is a blended curriculum in which the software component and the text components compliment one another. Your student will spend about 40% of class instructional time using computer-based tutorials and 60% using the *Student Text* to collaborate with peers and work with his or her teacher.

Students work at their own pace in the software component of the curriculum. The learning system is built on *cognitive models,* which represent the knowledge that a student might possess about the mathematics that they are studying. The software assesses students' prior mathematical knowledge on a step-by-step basis and presents problems tailored to their individual skill levels.

Using the Cognitive Tutor *Algebra I* software, your student will receive the benefits of individualized instruction, ample practice, immediate feedback, and coaching. Just-in-Time Hints, On-Demand Hints, and positive reinforcement will put your student in control of his or her own learning.

The Cognitive Tutor *Algebra I Student Text* offers lessons that parallel and extend the development of concepts in the software. The lessons emphasize written analyses and classroom presentations. Your student will engage in problem solving and reasoning, and will communicate using multiple representations of math concepts. The *Student Text* provides an opportunity for analysis, extended investigation, and the exploration of alternate solution paths. Real-world situations are used in problems designed to emphasize conceptual understanding. The goal of the *Student Text* is to be engaging and effective so your student will have fun while "Learning by Doing."

Introduction

A Closer Look at the Cognitive Tutor Algebra I Software

Skills for the Real World   Because people draw on basic mathematical reasoning skills for common tasks such as checking a paycheck, estimating the cost of a rental car, planning a garden, or choosing between long-distance telephone service carriers, these types of problems form the core of the Cognitive Tutor *Algebra I* software.

Monitoring and Feedback   The Cognitive Tutor *Algebra I* software monitors student activities as they work and provides them with feedback to individualize instruction. If a student makes an error, for example, the software will indicate why the answer is incorrect, or pose a thought-provoking question to redirect the student's reasoning. Through individualized feedback, the software keeps students on task, marks progress, and gives students a sense of accomplishment. The software also identifies areas in which a student is having difficulty and presents the student with problems that target those specific skills.

Optimizing Classroom Time   By individualizing instruction and targeting each student's strengths and weaknesses, the Cognitive Tutor *Algebra I* software can maximize the effectiveness of both the student's and the teacher's use of classroom time. The software immediately shows students whether their problem solving strategies and mathematical skills will be successful, allowing them to focus on correcting errors and developing skills that they find difficult. By using the diagnostic tools that accompany the software, teachers are free to interact with students on an individual basis and to target struggling students.

A Closer Look at the Cognitive Tutor Algebra I Student Text

Multiple Representations   Throughout the Cognitive Tutor *Algebra I* *Student Text*, deliberate connections are made between different representations in mathematics. For instance, students are shown that tables, graphs, and equations are different ways to represent functions.

Collaborative Learning Focus   The *Student Text* emphasizes the collaborative learning instruction model. Icons are placed at the beginning of problems in the lessons that encourage working in partner teams and in small groups. The instructional model icons are:

- ■ Discuss to Understand
- ■ Think for Yourself
- ■ Work with Your Partner
- ■ Work with Your Group
- ■ Share with the Class

A Typical Week in a Cognitive Tutor Algebra I Classroom

The Cognitive Tutor *Algebra I* classroom is a dynamic, adaptive environment. While no two weeks will be exactly the same in the Cognitive Tutor *Algebra I* classroom, most weeks will be split between classroom activities and work in the computer lab. The number of each type of session that the teacher schedules depends on the teacher's preference and the availability of lab time. Carnegie Learning suggests that students spend 40% of their class time in the computer lab working with the computer and 60% with *Student Text* investigations. Below is an itinerary outlining a typical mid-semester week.

Monday

- Students complete the *Student Text* investigation started on Friday with group presentations.

- Teacher solicits questions on the completed investigation and wraps up the investigation by asking questions that lead students to reflect on the material covered.

- Students begin a new *Student Text* investigation.

Tuesday

- Students complete about half of the investigation started on Monday.

- Teacher has students respond to a writing prompt to summarize their work.

Wednesday

- Students work with the software in the computer lab.

Thursday

- Students complete the investigation started on Tuesday.

- Partners present their findings of Tuesday's investigation using a written format.

- Teacher solicits questions and comments on the completed investigation, wraps up the investigation by asking questions that lead students to apply their knowledge of the material covered.

Friday

- Students work with the software in the computer lab.

How to Use the Homework Helper

The Homework Helper includes a practice page for each lesson in your student's *Student Text*. The page includes a worked example of the skills covered in the lesson. You may review the example with your student or have the student try the example without seeing the solution, and then review the example together.

Each page of the Homework Helper also has practice exercises that your student can try. The answers to the exercises are included at the back of the Homework Helper. Encourage your student to complete the solution before looking at the answer.

You can help your student to understand important mathematics vocabulary by reviewing the key words in a lesson.

Other Ways to Help Your Student

Encourage your student to share what he or she has been doing in mathematics class by showing you the lessons of his or her *Student Text*.

Support your student in completing his or her homework regularly by creating a consistent homework time each evening.

Use praise to encourage your student that he or she will succeed through persistent effort in working on the homework assignments.

Carnegie Learning's Ongoing Support

Teacher Training   Teacher Training gives educators the opportunity to understand the philosophy and application of the Carnegie Learning approach to mathematics. The training also provides important insights into the Cognitive Tutor *Algebra I* curriculum pedagogical, implementation, and assessment features.

Training sessions are conducted by Certified Implementation Specialists (CISs). Every CIS is a current or former mathematics teacher who has completed in-depth training from Carnegie Learning's staff of educators, technology specialists, and curriculum developers.

Family Math Night   Carnegie Learning offers families the opportunity to become involved through special programs such as our Family Math Night, in which parents come into their student's classroom to experience first-hand how the Cognitive Tutor *Algebra I* curriculum helps students learn mathematics. Students and their teachers work together to assist parents in solving mathematics problems using the Cognitive Tutor *Algebra I* software and *Student Text* investigation.

Contents

Contents

10 Polynomial Functions and Rational Expressions

11 Probability

12 Statistical Analysis

13 Quadratic and Exponential Functions and Logic

Designing a Patio
Patterns and Sequences

Students should be able to answer these questions after Lesson 1.1:

■ What is a sequence?

■ What is a term of a sequence?

■ How do I describe patterns of sequences?

Directions

Read Question 1 and its solution. Then, for Questions 2 and 3, use the sequence to find the correct answers.

1. Find the next two terms of the sequence and write a sentence describing the pattern.

Step 1   Find the next two terms.

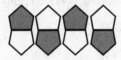 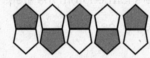

Step 2   Describe the pattern. The next term is found by starting with the previous figure and adding a column of pentagons to the right and shading the opposite pentagon.

2. The number of pentagons that make up each figure in the sequence above can form a sequence of numbers. Write this sequence of numbers.

3. What is the sixth term in the sequence you found in Question 2?

Find the next three terms in each sequence and write a sentence describing the pattern.

4. 96, 48, 24, _____, _____, _____

5. 3, 9, 27, _____, _____, _____

6. 35, 30, 25, _____, _____, _____

1.2 ■ Lemonade, Anyone?

Finding the 10th Term of a Sequence

Students should be able to answer these questions after Lesson 1.2:

■ What is a sequence and what is meant by the 10th term of a sequence?

■ What is a power?

■ What is the Order of Operations?

Directions

Read Question 1 and its solution. Then, use similar steps to complete Question 2.

1. You received $60 for your birthday. You are spending your money at the rate of $3 per day. Find how much money you have after 10 days.

   Step 1 Find how much money you have after 1 day. $60 - 3(1) = 57$

   Step 2 Find how much money you have after 2 days. $60 - 3(2) = 54$

   Step 3 Find how much money you have after 3 days. $60 - 3(3) = 51$

   Step 4 Write a sequence of numbers formed from the steps above. 60, 57, 54, 51, …

   Step 5 Find the 10th term of the sequence. $60 - 3(10) = 30$

   After 10 days, you will have $30 left.

2. You wake in the morning to find two inches of snow on the ground. The snow has been falling at a constant rate of one half inch per hour. Write a sequence representing the situation. What is the 10th term of the sequence? Explain what the 10th term represents.

Read Question 3 and its solution. Then, for Questions 4 and 5, perform the indicated operations. Show your work.

3. Simplify $3^2 + 4 \times 5$. Show your work.

   Step 1 Evaluate powers. $3^2 + 4 \times 5 = 9 + 4 \times 5$

   Step 2 Multiply. $9 + 4 \times 5 = 9 + 20$

   Step 3 Add. $9 + 20 = 29$

4. $(36 \div 4)^2 - 2^3$

5. $(27 - 6) + 18 \div 3$

Order of Operations

1. Evaluate expressions inside grouping symbols such as ( ) or [ ].

2. Evaluate powers.

3. Multiply and divide from left to right.

4. Add and subtract from left to right.

Dinner with the Stars
Finding the *n*th Term of a Sequence

Students should be able to answer these questions after Lesson 1.3:

■ What is an algebraic expression?

■ How do you evaluate an algebraic expression?

■ Why is the *n*th term of a sequence useful?

Directions

Read Question 1 and its solution. Then, use similar steps to complete Question 2.

1. You are making raspberry jam. Each jar of jam requires 0.75 cup of sugar. You can represent the cups of sugar needed to make different numbers of jars of jam with the sequence 0.75, 1.5, 2.25, …. How much sugar is needed to make 7 jars of jam? How much sugar is needed to make 12 jars of jam? What algebraic expression can you write to represent the amount of sugar needed for *n* jars of jam?

    Step 1   Total amount for 7 jars: 0.75(7) = 5.25 cups

    Step 2   Total amount for 12 jars: 0.75(12) = 9 cups

    Step 3   The number of jars is multiplied by 0.75, the amount to make one jar. The amount needed to make *n* jars is 0.75*n* cups.

2. You want to take swim lessons. There is a one-time pool maintenance fee of $25 and each lesson costs $10. The total cost for different numbers of lessons can be modeled by the sequence 35, 45, 55, …. How much does it cost to take 5 lessons? How much does it cost to take 15 lessons? Write an algebraic expression for the total cost of *n* lessons.

Read Question 3 and its solution. Then, answer Questions 4 and 5.

3. Evaluate $3x - 4$ when *x* is 3.

    Step 1   Substitute 3 for *x*. $3(3) - 4$

    Step 2   Simplify. $9 - 4 = 5$

4. Evaluate $4(m - 1)$ when *m* is 26.

5. Evaluate $3x^2$ when *x* is 6.

Read Question 6 and its solution. Then, for Questions 7 and 8, use the *n*th term to list the first three terms of each sequence. Show your work.

6. Use the *n*th term to list the first five terms of the sequence $a_n = 2n + 3$.

First term: $a_1 = 2(1) + 3 = 5$ Second term: $a_2 = 2(2) + 3 = 7$

Third term: $a_3 = 2(3) + 3 = 9$ Fourth term: $a_4 = 2(4) + 3 = 11$

Fifth term: $a_5 = 2(5) + 3 = 13$

7. $a_n = 5n - 4$ 8. $a_n = 3n^2 + 1$

1.4 Working for the CIA

Using a Sequence to Represent a Problem Situation

Students should be able to answer these questions after Lesson 1.4:
- How do you use a sequence of pictures to represent a problem situation?
- How do you use a sequence of numbers to represent a problem situation?

Directions

Read and solve Questions 1 through 5.

1. Chain letters are a method of communicating information to a large number of people. The person who writes the original chain letter may send it to 3 friends. The writer is the first link in the chain. The three people she sent it to are the second link. Each of them will copy the letter and send it to three more people, so that nine more copies of the letter are sent. In this problem situation, we want to find ways to represent the number of copies being made at different links in the chain. One way to represent this situation is with a picture. Continue the diagram below to represent the first 5 links in the chain. Indicate how many copies of the letter are made at Link 3, 4, and 5.

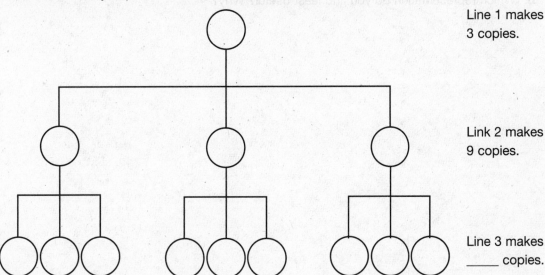

Line 1 makes 3 copies.

Link 2 makes 9 copies.

Line 3 makes _____ copies.

2. Another way to represent this situation is with a numeric sequence. Complete the table below. Then write a sequence for the first five links in the chain.

Link	1	2	3	4	5
Copies made	3	9			

Hint: 3   3 • 3   3 • 3 • 3

3. Another way to represent this situation is with words. Use a complete sentence to describe the pattern in the diagram and the table.

4. Another way to represent this situation is with an algebraic expression. Let *L* represent the link number. Write an algebraic expression that can be used to find the number of copies made at any link in the chain.

5. You have represented this problem situation with a picture, a sequence, a numeric sequence, words, and an expression.

   a. Which representation do you find most useful? Why?

   b. Which representation do you find least useful? Why?

1.5 Gauss' Formula

Finding the Sum of a Finite Sequence

Students should be able to answer these questions after Lesson 1.5:

■ What is Gauss' formula?

■ How can I write a formula for a pattern?

Directions

Read Question 1 and its solution. Then, answer Questions 2 through 5.

1. What is the sum of the numbers from 1 through 25?

   Step 1 Use Gauss' formula. $\dfrac{n(n + 1)}{2}$

   Step 2 Substitute 25 for n. $\dfrac{25(25 + 1)}{2}$

   Step 3 Simplify. $\dfrac{25(25 + 1)}{2} = \dfrac{25(26)}{2} = \dfrac{650}{2} = 325$

2. What is the sum of the numbers from 1 through 32?

3. What is the sum of the numbers from 1 through 75?

4. What is the sum of the numbers from 1 through 500?

5. What is the sum of the numbers from 1 through 1200?

6. Your intramural soccer league has 10 teams. During the regular season, each team will play every other team once. How many games will be played during the regular season?

7. Is Gauss' formula useful for answering Question 6? Why or why not? Use complete sentences in your answer.

1.6 $8 an Hour Problem
Using Multiple Representations, Part 1

Students should be able to answer these questions after Lesson 1.6:

■ What are some different ways to represent a problem situation?

■ How are the different representations related to each other?

■ What are the advantages and disadvantages of each representation?

Directions

Read Question 1 and its solution. Then, complete Questions 2 through 10.

1. This summer, your family is taking a road trip from Pittsburgh, PA to the Grand Canyon in Arizona. Your aunt will be doing all of the driving. She will drive at an average speed of 60 miles per hour. How far will she have driven after 5 hours?

   Step 1 Analyze the given information.

   You know the rate and time. You need to find distance. Distance = rate × time

   Step 2 Multiply. 60(5) = 300 miles

2. How far will your mom have driven after 15 hours? _____

3. Use a complete sentence to explain how you found your answers to Question 2.

4. How long will it take to drive 1200 miles? _____

5. Use a complete sentence to explain how you found your answers to Question 4.

6. The table below shows the number of hours that your mom drove during your 4-day trip to Arizona. Complete the table.

Labels	Day	Time spent driving	Distance traveled
Units		hours	miles
	Day 1	8	
	Day 2	10	
	Day 3	5	
	Day 4	7	

7. Use the bounds and intervals to label the grid. Then create a graph of the data from the table in Question 6.

Variable quantity	Lower bound	Upper bound	Interval
Time worked	0	30	2
Earnings	0	1800	100

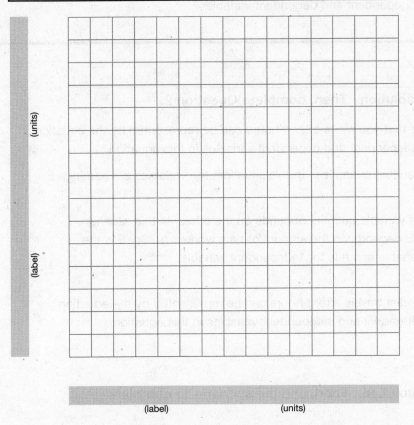

(units)

(label)

(label)   (units)

8. Use the graph to determine whether there is a number pattern in this problem. If there is a pattern, use compete sentences to describe the pattern.

9. Write an expression that you can use to find the distance traveled for any number of hours. Let *h* represent the number of hours spent driving. Use a complete sentence in your answer.

10. Suppose the distance you want to travel in one day is 550 miles. Write an algebraic equation for this situation using the expression you wrote in Question 9. Is 9 hours a solution of the equation? Write a complete sentence that explains your answer.

1.7 The Consultant Problem
Using Multiple Representations, Part 2

Students should be able to answer these questions after Lesson 1.7:
- Can you write an equation in two variables?
- What are independent and dependent variables?

Directions

Read Question 1 and its solution. Then, complete Question 2.

1. The amount of money E that you make after h hours can be represented by the equation $E = 10h$. Identify the independent and dependent variables in this equation.

   Step 1 Identify the variable quantities. In this situation, the variables are earnings E and hours h.

   Step 2 Identify which variable quantity depends on the other. In this situation, the earnings E depends on the amount of time worked h. So, E is the dependent variable and h is the independent variable.

2. The distance d that a cyclist travels after t hours can be represented by the equation $d = 30t$. Identify the dependent and independent variables in this equation.

Read Question 3 and its solution. Then, use the scenario to complete Questions 4 through 10.

3. You are carpeting your bedroom. Carpet costs $25 per square yard. How much would it cost if you need 189 square feet of carpet?

   Step 1 Change units of measure.

   $$189 \text{ ft}^2 \times \frac{\text{yd}^2}{9 \text{ ft}^2} = 21 \text{ yd}^2$$

   Step 2 Find the cost.

   $25(21) = 525$ It would cost $525 to carpet your bedroom.

> **Units of Measure**
>
> Remember that all similar measurements in a problem should be in the same units.

4. How much would it cost if you need 150 square feet of carpet?

5. The table below shows the cost of different amounts of carpeting. Complete the table.

Amount of carpet (square yards)	8	11	15	22	25
Cost (dollars)					

6. Create a graph of the data from the table in Question 5 on the grid.

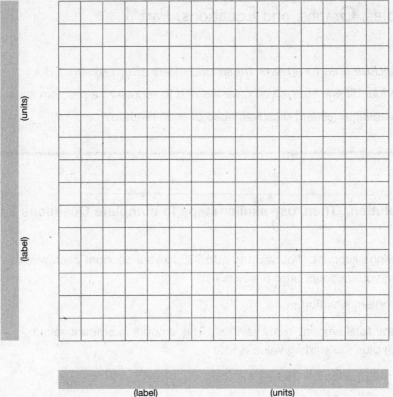

(units)

(label)

(label)   (units)

7. Write an expression that you could use to find the cost of any number of square yards of carpet. Let *x* represent the amount of carpet. Use a complete sentence in your answer.

8. Let *C* represent the cost in dollars. Write an equation that relates *C* and *x* for this problem situation. Use a complete sentence in your answer.

9. Determine which of the variable quantities in your equation in Question 8 depends on the other. Use complete sentences to explain your reasoning.

10. Identify the independent and dependent variables in your equation. Use a complete sentence in your answer.

1.8 U.S. Shirts
Using Tables, Graphs, and Equations, Part I

Students should be able to answer these questions after Lesson 1.8:

■ What are the four different ways you have learned to represent a problem situation?

■ What are the advantages and disadvantages of each method?

Directions

Read Question 1 and its solution. Then, use similar steps to complete Questions 2 and 3.

1. You have $183 in your savings account. You want to add $30 to your account each week. How much will you have in your account after 6 weeks?

   Step I   Describe the problem situation.

   I will calculate the total amount in my savings. This amount is amount saved each week ($30) plus the starting value ($183).

   Step 2   Total in dollars: 6(30) + 183 = 363

   After 6 weeks, I will have $363 in your savings account.

2. A storage company charges $100 to store your furniture in their warehouse plus an additional $35 per month. How much will they charge to rent their space for 3 months? Use a complete sentence in your answer.

3. A car rental company charges $30 to rent a car plus $.25 per mile. How much will they charge a customer that drives 200 miles? Use a complete sentence in your answer.

Use the scenario in Question 3 to answer Questions 4 through 8.

4. How much will the rental company charge a customer who drives 364 miles?

5. The rental company charges you $135.25 to rent a car. How many miles did you travel?

6. What are the two variable quantities in this problem situation? Assign letters to represent these quantities and include the units that are used to measure these quantities. Use a complete sentence in your answer.

7. Which of the variables from Question 6 is the independent variable and which is the dependent variable? Use a complete sentence in your answer.

8. Write an algebraic equation for the problem situation. Use a complete sentence in your answer.

1.9 Hot Shirts

Using Tables, Graphs, and Equations, Part 2

Students should be able to answer this question after Lesson 1.9:

■ How can you use estimation to determine an initial value when given a final result?

Directions

Read Question 1 and its solution. Then, use the scenario and similar steps to complete Questions 2 through 4.

1. Students in the school drama club are raising money to buy supplies for the school's spring musical. They have been working all year and have raised $100. Before winter break, they decided to sell candles as holiday gifts. For each candle sold, they will make $1.95. Estimate the number of candles sold if they raised a total of $150. Use a complete sentence in your answer.

    Step 1 Subtract what was already raised ($100) from the total ($150) to find how much was raised from selling the candles. Divide by the profit made from each candle to find how many candles were sold.

    $$\frac{150 - 100}{1.95} = \frac{50}{2} = 25$$

    Step 2 Write a complete sentence.

    If the drama club raised $150, then they sold approximately 25 candles

2. Estimate the number of candles sold if the club raised $200.

3. Estimate the number of candles sold if the club raised $380.

4. Estimate the number of candles sold if the club raised $1000.

5. Use your results from Questions 1–4 to complete a table of values for the problem situation.

Number of candles sold (candles)				
Amount raised (dollars)				

6. Write an algebraic equation for the problem situation.

1.10 Comparing U.S. Shirts and Hot Shirts
Comparing Problem Situations Algebraically and Graphically

Students should be able to answer these questions after Lesson 1.10:
- How do I compare two problem situations algebraically?
- How do I compare two problem situations graphically?

Directions

Read Question 1 and its solution. Then, use the scenario to complete Questions 2 through 7.

1. Two competing cell phone companies are offering special deals in your area. U R Connected charges $40 per month with no charges for the phone. Push My Buttons charges $35 per month and $100 for the phone. How much will each company charge for 5 months of service?

   Step 1 Total cost for U R Connected: 40(5) = 200

   Step 2 Total cost for Push My Buttons: 35(5) + 100 = 275

   Step 3 U R Connected will charge $200 for 5 months of service and Push My Buttons will charge $275 for 5 months of service. U R Connected gives a better price for 5 months or fewer.

2. How much will each company charge for 5 years (60 months) of service?

3. Use the grid to draw the graphs for the total cost for U R Connected and Push My Buttons.

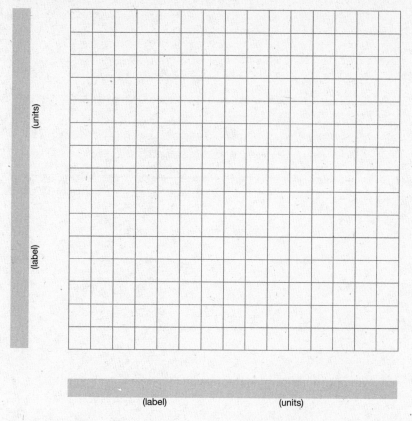

(units)

(label)

(label)   (units)

4. Use the graph to estimate the number of months of service for which the total costs are the same. Use a complete sentence in your answer.

5. For how many months of service is Push My Buttons more expensive? Use a complete sentence in your answer.

6. For how many months of service is U R Connected more expensive? Use a complete sentence in your answer.

7. Look back at your graph. Use sentences to describe the graphs in your own words.

2.1 Left-Handed Learners

Using Samples, Ratios, and Proportions to Make Predictions

Students should be able to answer these questions after Lesson 2.1:

- What is the difference between a ratio and a proportion?
- How are proportions used to make predictions based on a sample of a larger population?

Directions

Read Question 1 and its solution. Then, write the ratios in Questions 2 and 3.

1. You have a bag of marbles that contains 6 blue marbles, 3 yellow marbles, 8 red marbles, 12 purple marbles, and 5 green marbles. Write a ratio of the number of red marbles to the total number of marbles in the bag.

    Step 1   Find the total number of marbles.

    $6 + 3 + 8 + 12 + 5 = 34$

    Step 2   Find the ratio.

    $$\frac{\text{red marbles}}{\text{total marbles}} = \frac{8 \text{ marbles}}{34 \text{ marbles}}, \text{ or 8 marbles : 34 marbles}$$

2. Write a ratio of the number of yellow marbles to the number of purple marbles.

3. Write a ratio of the number of green marbles to the total number of marbles.

Read Question 4 and its solution. Then, use proportions to make predictions about the populations in Questions 5 and 6.

4. Three out of every four students in your school are members of an after school club. If there are 2000 students in your school, about how many are members of an after school club?

    Step 1   Let x represent the number of students in after school clubs.

    Step 2   Write and solve a proportion to predict the number of students in after school clubs.

    $$\frac{3}{4} = \frac{x}{2000}$$

    $4x = 3(2000)$

    $4x = 6000$

    $x = 1500$

There should be about 1500 students in after school clubs.

5. Two out of every 300 products made at a certain factory are defective. If 40 products are defective one week, about how many products were made that week?

6. You survey 10 dentists in your town and find that 8 of them recommend flossing after every meal. Which sampling method was used in your survey? Is the sample biased? Assume there are 40 dentists in your town. About how many of them recommend flossing after every meal?

Making Punch

Ratios, Rates, and Mixture Problems

Students should be able to answer these questions after Lesson 2.2:

- How do you use ratios to make comparisons?
- How are proportions used to solve mixture problems?

Directions

Read Question 1 and its solution. Then use the scenario to complete Question 2.

1. Your school cafeteria makes a fruit salad that is 5 parts strawberry and 7 parts banana. Suzie also makes a fruit salad that is 3 parts strawberry and 4 parts banana. Write a ratio that compares the number of parts of strawberry to the total number of parts for each recipe. Which recipe has the strongest taste of strawberry?

   Step 1   Find ratios.

   Cafeteria recipe: $\dfrac{5 \text{ parts strawberry}}{12 \text{ total parts}}$ Suzie's recipe: $\dfrac{3 \text{ parts strawberry}}{7 \text{ total parts}}$

   Step 2   Compare ratios.

   $\dfrac{5}{12} = \dfrac{35}{84}$ $\dfrac{3}{7} = \dfrac{36}{84}$;   So, $\dfrac{3}{7}$ is greater than $\dfrac{5}{12}$.

   Suzie's recipe has a stronger taste of strawberry.

2. Use similar steps to write a ratio that compares the number of parts of banana to the total number of parts for each recipe. Which recipe has the strongest taste of banana?

Read Question 3 and its solution. Then complete Question 4.

3. The cafeteria wants to give each student one cup of fruit salad. They plan to feed 540 students. Write a rate to find the number of cups of fruit salad there are in one part of the cafeteria recipe. How many cups of strawberries are needed to make enough fruit salad for the students?

   Step 1 $\dfrac{540 \text{ cups}}{12 \text{ parts}} = \dfrac{45 \text{ cups}}{1 \text{ part}}$

   Step 2 $\dfrac{45 \text{ cups}}{1 \text{ part}} = \dfrac{x}{5 \text{ parts}}$

              $x = 225$

   The cafeteria needs 225 cups of strawberries.

4. How many cups of bananas are needed to make enough fruit salad for the students?

2.3 Shadows and Proportions

Proportions and Indirect Measurement

Students should be able to answer these questions after Lesson 2.3:

- How do you use similar figures to write and solve proportions?
- What is a unit rate?

Directions

2 **Read Question 1 and its solution. Then, complete Questions 2 and 3.**

1. $\triangle ABC$ is similar to $\triangle DEF$. Use the diagram to find EF.

   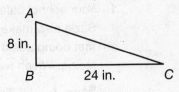

   Step 1   Write a proportion.

   $$\frac{AB}{DE} = \frac{BC}{EF}$$

   Step 2   Substitute and solve the proportion.

   $$\frac{8}{6} = \frac{24}{EF}$$

   $$8EF = 144$$

   $$EF = 18 \text{ in.}$$

   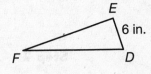

2. $\triangle ABC$ is similar to $\triangle DEF$. Find AB if $DE = 18$ cm, $BC = 7$ cm, and $EF = 9$ cm.

3. $\triangle JKL$ is similar to $\triangle MNO$. Find NO if $KL = 16$ mm, $MN = 18$ mm, and $JK = 24$ mm.

Read Question 4 and its solution. Then complete Questions 5 and 6.

4. Paul recorded the number of miles he drove his car for two months. He found that he drove a total of 1130 miles and used 45.2 gallons of gasoline. Write a unit rate that represents the number of miles the car traveled per gallon of gasoline.

   Step 1   Write the rate. $\dfrac{1130 \text{ miles}}{45.2 \text{ gallons}}$

   Step 2   Find the unit rate. $\dfrac{1130 \text{ miles}}{45.2 \text{ gallons}} = \dfrac{25 \text{ miles}}{1 \text{ gallon}}$

5. How many miles can Paul drive on 16 gallons of gasoline?

6. Paul paid $46.24 for 16 gallons of gasoline. Write a unit rate that represents the amount for one gallon of gasoline. How much would 25 gallons of gasoline cost?

2.4 TV News Ratings
Ratios and Part-to-Whole Relationships

Students should be able to answer these questions after Lesson 2.4:

■ How are ratios used to model part-to-whole relationships?

■ Can you write an equation that models a part-to-whole relationship?

Directions

Read Question 1 and its solution. Then, use the survey to complete Questions 2 through 8.

1. In a recent survey, it was found that 4 out of every 5 children brush their teeth twice a day. If 30 children were surveyed, how many brush their teeth twice a day?

   Step 1   Write an equation.

   $$\frac{4 \text{ children who brush}}{5 \text{ children}} = \frac{x \text{ children who brush}}{30 \text{ children}}$$

   Step 2   Solve the equation.

   $$5x = 120$$
   $$x = 24$$

   In the survey, 24 children brush their teeth twice a day.

2. How many children brush their teeth twice a day if 50 total children were surveyed?

3. How many children brush their teeth twice a day if 100 total children were surveyed?

4. How many children were surveyed if 120 said that they brush their teeth twice a day?

5. How many children were surveyed if 200 said that they brush their teeth twice a day?

6. Let c represent the number of children and let b represent the number of children that brush their teeth twice a day. Use the description to write an equation for b in terms of c.

   $$\frac{b}{c} = \frac{4}{5}$$

   _____ = _____   Set the means equal to the extremes.

   _____ = _____   Divide each side by 5.

7. Which variable from Question 6 is the independent variable and which variable is the dependent variable?

Women at a University

Ratios, Part-to-Part Relationships, and Direct Variation

Students should be able to answer these questions after Lesson 2.5:

■ How are part-to-part relationships used in problem-solving?

■ How are ratios used in direct variation problems?

Directions

2

Read Question 1 and its solution. Then, use the scenario to complete Questions 2 through 5.

1. Seven out of ten doctors at a local hospital are male. What is the ratio of the number of female doctors to the number of male doctors?

   Step 1   Find the number of female doctors.
   Because 7 out of 10 doctors are male, 3 must be female.

   Step 2   The ratio is $\dfrac{3 \text{ female doctors}}{7 \text{ male doctors}}$.

2. How many female doctors work at the hospital if there are 95 male doctors?

3. How many male doctors work at the hospital if there are 62 female doctors?

4. Let f represent the number of female doctors and let m represent the number of male doctors. Follow the instructions to write an equation for m in terms of f.

   $$\frac{f}{m} = \frac{?}{?}$$

   ____ = ____   Set the means equal to the extremes.

   $m =$ ____   Use mental math to solve for m.

5. Complete the table that represents the problem situation.

Labels	Female doctors	Male doctors
Units	doctors	doctors
Expressions	f	
	36	
		140
		224
	117	

2.6 Tipping in a Restaurant
Using Percents

Students should be able to answer these questions after Lesson 2.6:

- What is the relationship between percents and proportions?
- Can you find percents of numbers?

Directions

Read Question 1 and its solution. Then, complete Questions 2 through 4.

1. What is 35% of 20?

    Step 1   Rewrite 35% as a fraction.

    $$35\% = \frac{35}{100}$$

    Step 2   Solve a proportion.

    $$\frac{35}{100} = \frac{x}{20}$$

    $$100x = 700$$

    $$x = 7 \qquad \text{So, 7 is 35\% of 20.}$$

2. What is 20% of 30?

3. If 15% of a number is 30, what is the number?

4. If 25% of a number is 75, what is the number?

Read Question 5 and its solution. Then, complete Question 6.

5. The debate team is selling pencil cases to raise money to travel to the national debate championship in Washington DC. The club keeps 60% of the money they collect. Let c represent the money collected and let k represent the money the club keeps. Write an equation for k in terms of c. Do the variables in the equation have direct variation?

    Step 1   Write the equation. $k = \frac{60}{100}c$

    Step 2   The variables show direct variation because $\frac{60}{100}$ is a constant ratio.

6. All CD's at a music store are on sale for 75% of the regular price. Let r represent the regular price and let s represent the sale price. Write an equation for s in terms of r. Do the variables in the equation have direct variation? Use a complete sentence to explain your reasoning.

Percents and Taxes

Students should be able to answer these questions after Lesson 2.7:

- What is the relationship between percents and proportions?
- What is gross pay, net pay, and tax rate?

Directions

2

Read Question 1 and its solution. Then, complete Questions 2 through 8. Use complete sentences in your answers.

1. A department store is having a sale on sweaters. The regular price for a sweater is $35. After looking at your receipt, you see that you saved $5.25. What was the percent discount?

   Step 1   Write a proportion. $\dfrac{5.25}{35} = \dfrac{x}{100}$

   Step 2   Solve the proportion. $35x = 525$

   $x = 15$

   There was a 15% discount on the sweater.

2. How much did you pay for the sweater in Question 1? What percent of the regular price is this?

3. A worker earns a gross pay of $600 per week. Find the amount he pays in taxes if the tax rate is 37%.

4. Isabel paid $15,840 in taxes in one year. Find her gross pay if the tax rate is 33%.

5. A student answered 92% of the 75 test questions correctly. How many test questions did he answer correctly?

6. A serving of a soybean snack has 7 grams of protein. This is 14% of the protein that you should have in a day. How many grams of protein should you have a day?

7. Last year Philip's heating bill in November was $150. This year his bill in November went up by $45. By what percent did Philip's heating bill go up?

8. You would like to earn at least a B (80% or higher) on the upcoming history exam. If there are 40 questions on the exam, how many questions can you answer incorrectly?

© 2006 Carnegie Learning, Inc.

3.1 Collecting Road Tolls
Solving One-Step Equations

Students should be able to answer these questions after Lesson 3.1:

■ Can you write and solve one-step equations?

■ How do you check solutions to one-step equations algebraically and graphically?

Directions

Read Question 1 and its solution. Then for each equation in Questions 2 through 10, use a complete sentence to identify the operation you would use to get the variable by itself on one side of the equation. Then solve the equation and check the solution.

1. Solve the equation $x - 14 = 32$.

   Step 1   Add 14 to each side of the equation. Addition is the inverse operation of subtraction.

   Step 2   Solve the equation.

   $$x - 14 = 32$$
   $$x - 14 + 14 = 32 + 14$$
   $$x = 46$$

   Step 3   Check the solution.

   $$x - 14 = 36$$
   $$46 - 14 \stackrel{?}{=} 32$$
   $$32 = 32$$

2. $x + 11 = 26$

3. $x - 7 = 31$

4. $4x = 36$

5. $\dfrac{x}{7} = 12$

6. $x + 47 = 98$

7. $x - 34 = 51$

8. $8.5 = \dfrac{x}{9}$

9. $3x = 561$

10. $74 + x = 218$

Read the problem scenario below. Use the scenario to complete Questions 11 through 14.

Carla has been offered a babysitting job at her neighbor's house. She will be paid $9 per hour.

11. How much money will Carla make in 3 hours?

© 2006 Carnegie Learning, Inc.

12. Let h represent the number of hours Carla works. Write an algebraic expression that represents the amount of money she earns.

13. Carla would like to buy a bicycle that costs $108. Write and solve an equation to find the number of hours she must work to earn enough to buy the bicycle.

14. Explain how inverse operations helped you solve the equation in Question 13.

Decorating the Math Lab

Solving Two-Step Equations

Students should be able to answer these questions after Lesson 3.2:

- Can you solve two-step equations?
- How do you check solutions to two-step equations algebraically and graphically?

Directions

Read Question 1 and its solution. Then for each equation in Questions 2 through 10, use a complete sentence to identify the operations you would use to get the variable by itself on one side of the equation and the order in which you would perform these operations. Then solve the equation and check the solution.

1. Solve the equation $3x - 1 = 20$.

   Step 1 Add 1 to each side of the equation. Addition is the inverse operation of subtraction.

   Then divide each side of the equation by 3. Division is the inverse operation of multiplication.

   Step 2 Solve the equation.

   $$3x - 1 = 20$$
   $$3x = 21$$
   $$x = 7$$

   Step 3 Check the solution

   $$3x - 1 = 20$$
   $$3(7) - 1 \stackrel{?}{=} 20$$
   $$20 = 20$$

2. $\dfrac{x}{4} - 6 = 0$

3. $5x + 3 = 38$

4. $4x - 8 = 24$

5. $\dfrac{x}{3} + 7 = 11$

6. $9 + 6x = 63$

7. $\dfrac{x}{5} - 3 = 18$

8. $51 = 3x - 12$

9. $42 = 16 + \dfrac{x}{2}$

10. $19 = \dfrac{x}{6} - 1$

Read the problem scenario below. Use the scenario to complete Questions 11 through 13.

Sonya is planning a dinner party. She found a caterer that charges $12.50 per person plus $150 for the rental of the hall.

11. How much will the dinner party cost if Sonya invites 30 people? _____

    How much will the dinner party cost if Sonya invites 50 people? _____

12. Let p represent the number of people invited. Write an algebraic expression that represents the total cost of the dinner party.

13. Sonya wants to spend a maximum of $1400. Use your expression to write an equation that can be used to find the number of guests Sonya can invite for $1400. Solve the equation and write your answer in a complete sentence.

3.3 Earning Sales Commission
Using the Percent Equation

Students should be able to answer these questions after Lesson 3.3:
- What is the percent equation?
- Can you write and solve two-step percent equations?

Directions

Read Question 1 and its solution. Then, in Questions 2 through 4, write and solve a percent equation to answer each question. Use a complete sentence in your answer.

1. Write and solve a percept equation to answer the question below. Use a complete sentence in your answer.

   225 is what percent of 500?

   Step 1 Write the percent equation. $a = \dfrac{p}{100}b$

   Step 2 Substitute 225 for *a* and 500 for *b*. $225 = \dfrac{p}{100}(500)$

   Step 3 Solve for *p*. $p = 45\%$

   Step 4 Write a sentence.   The number 225 is 45% of 500.

2. 11 is what percent of 20?   3. 36 is what percent of 48?   4. What is 30% of 580?

Read Question 5 and its solution. Then complete Questions 6 and 7.

5. Marcus works as a salesperson at a department store. He earns a base salary of $200 per week plus a commission that is 5% of his total sales. How much money will he earn if his total sales are $375?

   Step 1 Find his earnings from commission.   0.05(375) = 18.75

   Step 2 Add his base salary.   18.75 + 200 = 218.75

   Marcus will earn $218.75.

6. How much money will he earn if his total sales are $2000? Use a complete sentence in your answer.

7. Let *t* represent Marcus' total sales and let *E* represent his earnings. Write an equation for his earnings in terms of his total sales. Use your equation to find Marcus' total sales if his earnings are $375.

Students should be able to answer these questions after Lesson 3.4:

■ Can you write and solve two-step equations?

■ Can you use equations, tables, and graphs to find the better deal?

Directions

Use the scenario below to complete Questions 1 through 7.

You are trying to decide which local fitness center to join. Fitness Place charges a membership fee of $75 plus $40 per month. Slim Chance, a fitness center specializing in aerobic workouts, charges a membership fee of $150 plus $30 per month.

1. What will the cost be for 5 months at each gym?

Step 1	Calculate cost for Fitness Place.	$40(5) + 75 = 200 + 75 = 275$
		It costs $275 for 5 months at Fitness Place.
Step 2	Calculate cost for Slim Chance.	$30(5) + 150 = 150 + 150 = 300$
		It costs $300 for 5 months at Slim Chance.

2. Complete the table showing the cost for each fitness center.

	Fitness Place		Slim Chance	
Labels	Time	Total cost	Time	Total cost
Units	months	dollars	months	dollars
Expressions	t		t	
	0		0	
	5	275	5	300
	15		15	
	20		20	

3. Which fitness center is the better deal if you want to be a member for 3 months?
    Which fitness center is the better deal if you want to be a member for 12 months?

4. Let c represent the total cost of the gym membership and let t represent the number of months of the membership. Write an equation that gives the total cost in terms of the number of months of the membership for each fitness center.

5. The total cost of a gym membership at each fitness center is given below. Use the equations you wrote in Question 4 to find the number of months purchased.

a. Fitness Place: $2475

b. Slim Chance: $1230

6. Use the bounds and intervals shown below to create graphs of the two situations on the grid.

Variable quantity	Lower bound	Upper bound	Interval
Months purchased	0	60	4
Total cost	0	2700	180

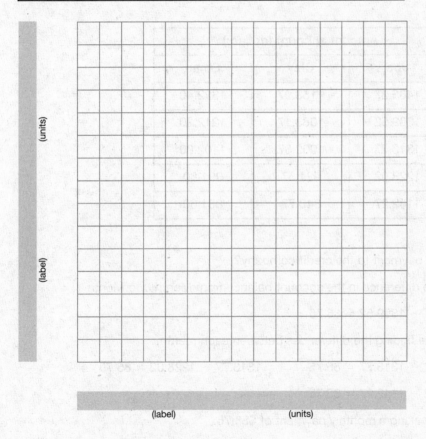

(units)

(label)

(label)   (units)

7. Compare the two fitness centers' prices. Write a paragraph that indicates which fitness center will cost the least and for which numbers of months. Can you tell whether the cost will ever be the same for the two centers? If so, for which number of months will the cost be the same? Use complete sentences to explain.

Students should be able to answer these questions after Lesson 3.5:

■ Can you write and solve two-step equations?

■ Can you compare three problem situations?

Directions

Use the problem scenario below to complete Questions 1 through 6.

Joe, Clay, and Ethan each opened a credit account with no interest for 1 year. They are each making regular payments to the credit company to try to pay off the account before getting charged with interest. The table below shows the balance in the account after making a payment each month.

Number of months	Amount account (dollars)		
	Joe	Clay	Ethan
0	1485.27	1163.97	1322.40
1	1399.52	1083.17	1212.20
2	1313.77	1002.37	1102.00
3	1228.02	921.57	991.80
4	1142.27	840.77	881.60

1. What is Joe's monthly payment to the credit company?

   Step 1   Find the difference in the account balance from Month 0 to Month 1.

   $1485.27 - 1399.52 = 85.75$

   Step 2   Continue finding the differences between each month.

   $1399.52 - 1313.77 = 85.75$ $1313.77 - 1228.02 = 85.75$

   $1228.02 - 1142.27 = 85.75$

   Joe is making a monthly payment of $85.75.

2. What are Clay and Ethan's monthly payments to the credit company?

3. What is the balance in each account after 12 months? Are all the accounts paid off? If not, which accounts still have a balance?

4. Let *m* represent the number of months and let *b* represent the balance of the account.

    a. Write an equation that gives the balance of Joe's account in terms of the number of months.

    b. Write an equation that gives the balance of Clay's account in terms of the number of months.

    c. Write an equation that gives the balance of Ethan's account in terms of the number of months.

5. Use the bounds and intervals shown below to create graphs for each person's account balance in terms of the number of months.

Variable quantity	Lower bound	Upper bound	Interval
Months	0	15	1
Balance	0	1500	100

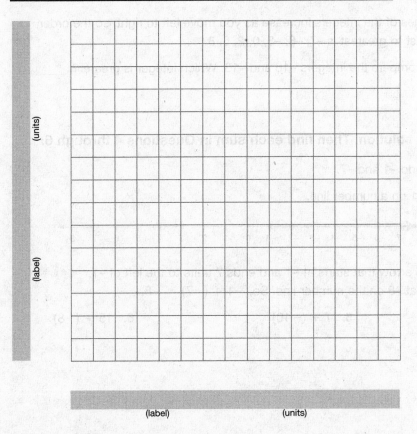

(units)

(label)

(label)   (units)

6. Clay's beginning balance is the lowest. Find the number of months for which his account balance is the lowest. Use complete sentences to explain why his balance is not always the lowest.

Brrr! It's Cold Out There!

Integers and Integer Operations

Students should be able to answer these questions after Lesson 3.6:

- Can you compare integers using a number line?
- Can you add, subtract, multiply, and divide positive and negative integers?

Directions

Read Question 1 and its solution. Then complete Question 2.

1. Use a number line to write the following integers in order from least to greatest.

   –6, 5, 8, 2, –3, 0, –7

   Step 1   Graph the numbers on a number line.

   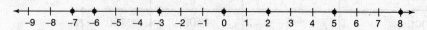

   Step 2   The values of the integers increase as you move left to right, so the order from least to greatest is –7, –6, –3, 0, 2, 5, 8.

2. Use a number line to compare the integers –16 and –13. Which integer is greater?

Read Question 3 and its solution. Then find each sum in Questions 4 through 6.

3. Use a number line to add –1 and –7.

   Step 1   Graph –1 on a number line.

   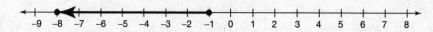

   Step 2   Draw an arrow that starts at –1 and ends 7 units to the left of –1. You are at –8 on the number line. So, $-1 + (-7) = -8$.

4. $-4 + (-2)$

5. $7 + (-10)$

6. $15 + (-8)$

Read Question 7 and its solution. Then find each difference in Questions 8 through 10.

7. Use a number line to subtract –3 from 6.

    Step 1   Graph 6 on a number line.

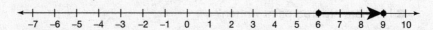

    Step 2   Draw an arrow that starts at 6 and ends 3 units to the right of 6.
                  You are at 9 on the number line. So, 6 – (–3) = 9.

8. 2 – (–6)   9. –5 – (–10)   10. –13 – (–7)

Read Question 11 and its solution. Then perform the indicated operation in Questions 12 through 14.

11. Find the product of 5 and –6.

    Step 1   The product of a positive integer and a negative integer is a negative
                  integer. So, 5(–6) = –30.

12. –3(–8)   13. –54 ÷ 9   14. –36 ÷ (–12)

3.7 Shipwreck at the Bottom of the Sea

The Coordinate Plane

Students should be able to answer these questions after Lesson 3.7:

■ How are ordered pairs written?

■ Can you plot points in a coordinate plane?

Directions

Read Question 1 and its solution. Then use the coordinate plane to write the ordered pair that corresponds to each point in Questions 2 through 5.

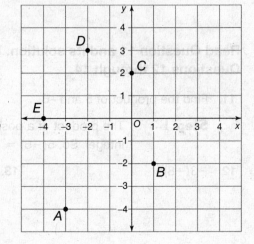

1. Write the ordered pair that corresponds to point *A* in the coordinate plane at the right.

   Step 1   The point is 3 units to the left of the origin, so the *x*-coordinate is –3.

   Step 2   The point is 4 units down from the origin, so the *y*-coordinate is –4.

   Step 3   The ordered pair corresponding to *A* is (–3, –4).

2. Point *B*

3. Point *C*

4. Point *D*

5. Point *E*

Read Question 6 and its solution. Then, use the coordinate plane to plot the ordered pairs in Questions 7 through 11.

6. Plot and label the point *A*(2, –4) in the coordinate plane at the right.

   Step 1   Start at the origin. Move 2 units to the right and 4 units down.

   Step 2   Label the point.

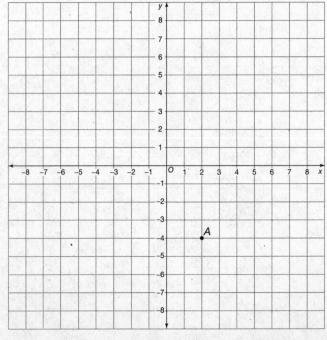

7. *B*(0, 5)

8. *C*(–1, –8)

9. *D*(–6, 4)

10. *E*(2, 3)

11. *F*(5, 0)

3.8 Engineering a Highway
Using a Graph of a Two-Step Equation

Students should be able to answer these questions after Lesson 3.8:

■ Can you write and use a two-step equation?

■ Can you use a graph to estimate solutions to equations?

Directions

Read Question 1 and its solution. Then, use the scenario to complete Questions 2 through 9. Use complete sentences in your answers.

1. You are riding up in a hot air balloon. It has been ascending at a constant rate of 10.5 feet per minute since the trip started. When you reached a height of 300 feet, you started a log to track your height. Write an equation that represents the height of the balloon in terms of the number of minutes since you started the log. Then find the height of the balloon in 10 minutes.

   Step 1 The balloon is currently at a height of 300 feet. The balloon's rate of change is 10.5 feet per minute. So, an equation is $h = 10.5m + 300$, where h is the height and m is the number of minutes since you started the log.

   Step 2 $h = 10.5(10) + 300 = 405$

   In 10 minutes, you will be at a height of 405 feet in the air.

2. What is the height of the balloon in 1 hour?

3. How many minutes it will take to reach a height of 468 feet?

4. How many minutes ago was the balloon at a height of 100 feet?

5. How many minutes before you started keeping a log did you begin your balloon ride?

6. Complete the table of values that shows the relationship between the number of minutes and the height of the balloon.

Labels	Time	Height of balloon
Units	minutes	feet
Expressions	m	
	−10	
	0	
	10	
	30	

7. Use the bounds and the grid below to create a graph of the data from the table.

Variable quantity	Lower bound	Upper bound	Interval
Time	−60	60	8
Height of balloon	0	1200	80

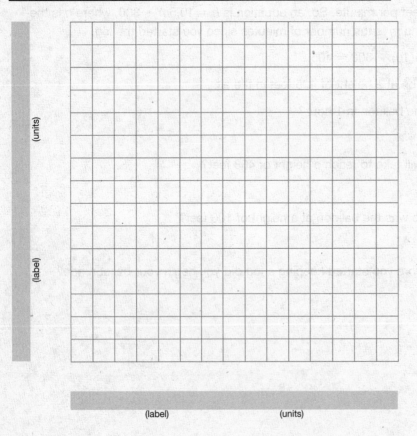

(units)

(label)

(label)   (units)

8. Use your graph to estimate when the balloon will be at a height of 700 feet. Use a complete sentence in your answer.

3

4.1 Up, Up, and Away!

Solving and Graphing Inequalities in One Variable

Students should be able to answer these questions after Lesson 4.1:

- Can you write simple and compound inequalities?
- Can you solve and graph inequalities?

Directions

Read Question 1 and its solution. Then, complete Questions 2 and 3.

1. One employer requires that the employees work at least 20 hours but no more than 40 hours per week to be eligible for health insurance benefits. Represent the number of hours that the employees must work using an inequality. Then graph the inequality.

   Step 1 The number of hours should include 20 and 40 and all values in between. The inequality is $20 \le x \le 40$.

   Step 2 Graph the inequality $20 \le x \le 40$.

   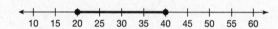

2. A family is saving money to remodel their bathroom. They estimated that the job would cost between $4000 and $7500. Represent the range of costs using an inequality. Then graph the inequality.

3. Lydia is permitted to watch no more than 10 hours of television per week. Write an inequality showing the number of hours that Lydia is allowed to watch television. Then graph the inequality.

Read Question 4 and its solution. Then solve and graph each inequality in Questions 5 through 7.

4. Solve the inequality $-3x + 2 > 8$ and then graph the solution.

   Step 1 $-3x + 2 > 8$

   $-3x > 6$ Subtract 2 from each side.

   $x < -2$ Divide each side by –3. Reverse the inequality symbol.

Step 2

5. $2x - 5 \leq 7$

6. $-4x < -32$

7. $\dfrac{x}{2} + 4 > -1$

8. In training for the Olympics, a long-distance runner estimated that she should run more than 70 miles per week. She has run 43 miles so far this week. Write and solve an inequality that describes the possible miles she should run to meet her goal for the week.

Moving a Sand Pile

Relations and Functions

Students should be able to answer these questions after Lesson 4.2:

- How do you determine whether a relation is a function?
- Can you determine the domain and range of a function?

Directions

Read Question 1 and its solution. Then use the scenario to complete Questions 2 through 4.

1. A scuba diver begins ascending toward the surface from a depth of 102 feet. The diver ascends at a rate of 3 feet per second. The equation $y = -102 + 3x$ represents the depth of the diver in terms of the time in seconds. Find the amount of time it takes the diver to reach a depth of 45 feet.

   Step 1   Write an equation. $-45 = -102 + 3x$

   Step 2   Solve the equation. $57 = 3x$

   $19 = x$

   It takes the diver 19 seconds to reach a depth of 45 feet.

2. Complete the table of values that describes the relationship between the depth of the diver and the amount of time.

Labels	Time	Depth
Units	seconds	feet
Expressions	x	$-102 + 3x$
	0	
		−81
	19	−45
		0

3. Write the ordered pairs given by the values in the table in Question 2.

4. Identify the inputs and outputs of the relation given by the ordered pairs in Question 3.

Read Question 5 and its solution. Then in Questions 6 and 7, decide whether each relation is a function. If the relation is a function, identify the domain and range. If the relation is not a function, explain why.

5. Is the following relation a function?　　　　Relation: (–4, –7), (–3, –5), (0, 1), (1, 3), (1, 5)

Step 1　　Identify the input values: –4, –3, 0, and 1

Step 2　　Check to see if any input value has more than one output value. In this relation, the input value 1 has two output values, 3 and 5. So, this relation is not a function.

6. Relation: (–3, 2), (0, 0), (2, 0), (4, –1), (5, 2)　　　7. Relation: (4, 2), (4, 1), (6, 7), (4, 3), (–3, 0)

4.3 Let's Bowl

Evaluating Functions, Function Notation, Domain, and Range

Students should be able to answer these questions after Lesson 4.3:
- How are functions evaluated?
- What is function notation?

Directions

Read Question 1 and its solution. Then, in Questions 2 though 5, evaluate each function at the specified value.

1. Evaluate $f(x) = 2x - 1$ at $x = 2$.

   Step 1   Replace x with the value of 2. $f(2) = 2(2) - 1$

   Step 2   Simplify. $= 4 - 1$

   $= 3$

2. $f(x) = 7x$ at $x = -8$

3. $g(x) = -4x + 11$ at $x = -5$

4. $h(x) = 8x + 5$ at $x = -4$

5. $f(x) = x^2 - 3x$ at $x = 1$

Read Question 6 and its solution. Then, complete Questions 7 and 8.

6. To fix your car, it is going to cost you $468 for parts plus $36 per hour for labor. The cost can be represented by the equation $y = 36x + 468$. The mechanic estimates it will take at most 4 hours to repair the car. What is the domain and range of this function?

   Step 1   To find the domain, determine which values of x make sense in this problem situation. The domain is {1, 2, 3, 4}.

   Step 2   To find the range, evaluate the function at each value in the domain. The range is {504, 540, 576, 612}.

7. What is the domain and range of the function in Question 6 if you do not consider the problem situation?

8. Consider the function $f(x) = 6x - 10$. For each of the following domains, find the corresponding range of the function.

   a. Domain: {1, 2, 3, 4, ...}

   b. Domain: {all real numbers}

   c. Domain: {-6, -3, 0, 3, 6}

Math Magic

The Distributive Property

Students should be able to answer these questions after Lesson 4.4:

■ How is the distributive property used to factor expressions?

■ How is the distributive property used to simplify expressions?

Directions

Read Question 1 and its solutions. Then, in Questions 2 through 7 use the distributive property to simplify each expression.

1. Use the distributive property to simplify each expression.

   a. $8(73) = 8(70 + 3) = 8(70) + 8(3) = 560 + 24 = 584$

   b. $\dfrac{36 - 18}{6} = \dfrac{36}{6} - \dfrac{18}{6} = 6 - 3 = 3$

2. $8(99)$

3. $4(5x + 1)$

4. $\dfrac{15 - 6x}{3}$

Read Question 5 and its solutions. Then, in Questions 6 through 8 use the distributive property to factor the greatest common factor from each expression. Then simplify the expression.

5. Use the distributive property to factor the greatest common factor from each expression. Then simplify the expression.

   a. $4x + 32 = 4x + 4(8) = 4(x + 8)$

   b. $42x - 12x = 6x(7) - 6x(2) = 6x(7 - 2) = 6x(5) = 30x$

6. $6x - 9$

7. $5x + 35x$

8. $16x - 40x$

9. Write two expressions for the total area of the two rectangles below. Then find the total area if $x = 15$ feet.

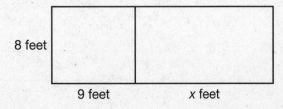

4.5 Numbers in Your Everyday Life

Real Numbers and Their Properties

Students should be able to answer these questions after Lesson 4.5:

■ What are the different types of real numbers?

■ What are the properties of real numbers?

Directions

Read Question 1 and its solution. Then, in Questions 2 through 4, classify each number as a rational number, irrational number, integer, whole number, or natural number. There may be more than one correct answer. The Venn Diagram in section 4.5 of the student text will be helpful in answering these questions.

1. Classify 0 as a rational number, irrational number, integer, whole number, or natural number.

   Step 1   Zero is a whole number. From the Venn Diagram, you can see that whole numbers are also integers and rational numbers. So, zero is classified as a whole number, integer, and rational number.

2. −32

3. $\dfrac{5}{6}$

4. π

In Questions 5 through 8, match the property that is illustrated with its name.

5. $5 + 0 = 5$

6. $-150 + 150 = 0$

7. $123 \times 1 = 123$

8. $6 \times \dfrac{1}{6} = 1$

A. Multiplicative Identity

B. Additive Identity

C. Multiplicative Inverse

D. Additive Inverse

In Question 9, identify the property that is used in each step of solving the equation. The first step is done as an example.

9.

$5(2x + 3) = 3(9 + 6) - 27$	Given problem
$10x + 15 = 27 + 18 - 27$	Distributive Property of Multiplication Over Addition
$10x + 15 = 27 - 27 + 18$	_____
$10x + 15 = 0 + 18$	_____
$10x + 15 = 18$	_____
$10x + 15 - 15 = 18 - 15$	_____
$10x = 3$	_____
$\dfrac{10x}{10} = \dfrac{3}{10}$	_____
$x = 0.3$	_____

Technology Reporter
Solving More Complicated Equations

Students should be able to answer these questions after Lesson 4.6:

■ Can you solve equations with variables on both sides?

■ Can you represent a problem situation with an equation that has variables on both sides?

Directions

Read Question 1 and its solution. Then, in Questions 2 through 4 solve each equation and check your answers.

1. Solve $2x + 1 = x - 5$.

    Step 1   Isolate the variable on one side of the equation.

    $$2x + 1 = x - 5$$

    $$2x - x + 1 = x - x - 5 \quad \text{Subtract } x \text{ from each side.}$$

    $$x + 1 = -5$$

    $$x + 1 - 1 = -5 - 1 \quad \text{Subtract 1 from each side.}$$

    $$x = -6$$

    Step 2   Check your answer in the original equation.

    $$2x + 1 \stackrel{?}{=} x - 5$$

    $$2(-6) + 1 \stackrel{?}{=} -6 - 5$$

    $$-11 = -11$$

2. $8(4x - 1) = 24x$ 3. $3x - 5 = 4(2x - 5)$ 4. $6(3x - 3) = -9(x + 8)$

5. Gabrielle has been offered two summer jobs. The first job is a lifeguard position that will pay $11 per hour but requires that she take a $200 certification class. The second job is a waitress position at a local restaurant. This job pays $9 per hour, but she will have to buy a uniform for $50. Gabrielle decides to make a few calculations concerning the money that can be made before deciding which job to take.

    a. Let x represent the number of hours worked. Write an expression that represents the money earned from the lifeguard position.

    b. Let x represent the number of hours worked. Write an expression that represents the money earned from the waitress position.

    c. After how many hours will Gabrielle earn the same amount of money from both jobs?

4.7 Rules of Sports

Solving Absolute Value Equations and Inequalities

Students should be able to answer these questions after Lesson 4.7:

- Can you solve absolute value equations?
- Can you solve and graph absolute value inequalities?

Directions

Read Question 1 and its solution. Then, evaluate each expression in Questions 2 though 4.

1. Evaluate the expression $|-9| + |-3|$.

   Step 1 Evaluate the expression inside the absolute value symbols first then simplify.

   $|-9| + |-3| = 9 + 3 = 12$

2. $|-11 - 6|$

3. $|(-8)(-4)|$

4. $\dfrac{|-27|}{|3|}$

Read Question 5 and its solution. Then, solve each absolute value equation in Questions 6 though 8.

5. Solve the equation $|2x + 3| = 11$.

   Step 1 Set the expression inside the absolute value symbols equal to –11 and 11.

   $2x + 3 = 11$ or $2x + 3 = -11$

   Step 2 Solve each equation.

$2x + 3 = 11$		$2x + 3 = -11$
$2x = 8$		$2x = -14$
$x = 4$	or	$x = -7$

6. $|7 - x| = 25$

7. $|3x + 1| = 16$

8. $|2x - 13| = 7$

Read Question 9 and its solution. Then, in Questions 10 and 11 solve each absolute value inequality and graph your solution on the number line.

9. Solve $|x + 3| \leq 6$ and graph the solution on a number line.

   Step 1 The equivalent inequality is $-6 \leq x + 3 \leq 6$.

   Step 2 Solve the inequality.

   $-6 \leq x + 3 \leq 6$

   $-9 \leq \quad x \quad \leq 3$

Step 3   Graph the solution.

$$\underset{-10\;-8\;-6\;-4\;-2\;\;0\;\;2\;\;4\;\;6\;\;8\;\;10}{\xleftarrow{\hspace{1cm}} \bullet \underset{-9}{} \rule{2cm}{0.4pt} \bullet \underset{3}{} \xrightarrow{\hspace{1cm}}}$$

10. $|2x - 5| > 9$

$\xleftarrow{\hspace{6cm}}\rightarrow$

11. $|x| - 4 \geq 6$

$\xleftarrow{\hspace{6cm}}\rightarrow$

Widgets, Dumbbells, and Dumpsters

Multiple Representations of Linear Functions

Students should be able to answer this question after Lesson 5.1:

■ Can you represent a linear function using an equation, a table, and a graph?

Directions

Read Question 1 and its solution. Then, use the problem scenario to complete Questions 2 through 8.

1. Katie is going bowling. The bowling alley charges $3 to rent shoes and $1.50 for every game played. Katie needs to rent shoes. How much will she pay to play 4 games?

    Step 1   Multiply the number of games by the cost to play one game.

    $4(1.5) = 6$

    Step 2   Add the cost to rent shoes.

    $6 + 3 = 9$

    Katie will pay $9 to play 4 games at the bowling alley.

2. Write an equation that gives the total cost in terms of the number of games played. Use *x* to represent the number of games and use *y* to represent the total cost in dollars.

3. Use your equation to find the total cost of 7 games.

4. Katie has $15. Use your equation to find the number of games she can play.

5. Complete the table of values that shows the relationship between the total cost and the number of games.

Labels	Games	Total cost
Units	games	dollars
Expressions	*x*	
	1	
		7.5
	5	
		18

6. Use the grid below to create a graph of the data from the table on the previous page. First, choose your bounds and intervals.

Variable quantity	Lower bound	Upper bound	Interval
Games			
Total cost			

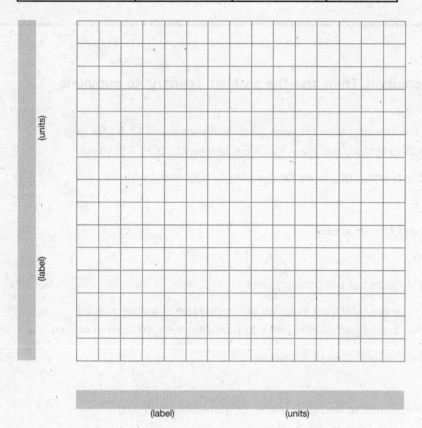

(units)

(label)

(label)   (units)

7. Use your graph to approximate the total cost of playing 12 games. Then explain how you found your answer, using complete sentences.

8. Use your graph to approximate the number of games that can be played for $25. Then explain how you found your answer, using complete sentences.

5

5.2 Selling Balloons

Finding Intercepts of a Graph

Students should be able to answer these questions after Lesson 5.2:

■ How do you find the intercepts of a graph?

■ Can you interpret the meaning of intercepts in a problem situation?

Directions

Read Question 1 and its solution. Then, algebraically find the intercepts of the graph of each equation in Questions 2 and 3.

1. Algebraically find the intercepts of the graph of the equation $y = -2x + 10$.

   Step 1 To find the x-intercept, let $y = 0$ and solve for x.

   $$0 = -2x + 10$$
   $$-10 = -2x$$
   $$5 = x$$

   The x-intercept is 5. So, the graph crosses the x-axis at the point (5, 0).

   Step 2 To find the y-intercept, let $x = 0$ and solve for 5.

   $$y = -2(0) + 10 = 10$$

   The y-intercept is 10. So, the graph crosses the y-axis at (0, 10).

2. $y = 4x - 20$

3. $y = -3x - 9$

4. A shoe store has 56 pairs of a popular brand of shoe in stock. During a sale, the store sold an average of 7 pairs every day. Write an equation for the problem situation. Let x represent the number of days and let y represent the number of pairs of shoes in stock. Then find the x- and y-intercepts. What do the intercepts mean in this problem situation?

© 2006 Carnegie Learning, Inc.

5

Recycling and Saving
Finding the Slope of a Line

Students should be able to answer these questions after Lesson 5.3:

■ How is unit rate calculated in a problem situation?

■ Can you find the slope of a line given two points on the line?

Directions

Read Question 1 and its solution. Then, find the unit rate for each situation in Questions 2 and 3.

1. Pizza is being sold as a fundraiser in the school cafeteria. Three slices will cost the teachers $2.25. What is the unit rate? What is the cost of 5 slices of pizza?

   Step 1   The unit rate is the cost of 1 piece of pizza.

   Unit rate: $\dfrac{\$2.25}{3 \text{ slices}} = \dfrac{\$.75}{1 \text{ slice}}$

   For every slice of pizza bought, the cost will increase by $.75.

   Step 2 $\dfrac{\$.75}{1 \text{ slice}} \times 5 \text{ slices} = \$3.75$

   It will cost $3.75 for 5 slices of pizza.

2. During their cross-country road trip, the Jenkins family traveled 1620 miles in 3 days. What is the unit rate?

3. Margaret can run 3 miles in 30 minutes. What is the unit rate? How far can Margaret run in 45 minutes?

Read Question 4 and its solution. Then, find the slope of the line through the points in Questions 5 through 7.

4. Find the slope of the line through the points (–1, 3) and (2, 9).

   Step 1   Use the formula for slope.

   $$m = \frac{\text{rise}}{\text{run}} = \frac{y_2 - y_1}{x_2 - x_1}$$

   Step 2   Substitute values and simplify.

   $$= \frac{9 - 3}{2 - (-1)} = \frac{6}{3} = 2$$

   The slope of the line through (–1, 3) and (2, 9) is 2.

   Note

   If a student has difficulty calculating slope, plot the points on a graph and count the changes in *y*- and *x*-values from one point to the next.

5. (0, 0) and (1, –2)

6. (2, –1) and (4, 0)

7. (1, 7) and (5, –5)

5.4 Running in a Marathon

Slope-Intercept Form

Students should be able to answer these questions after Lesson 5.4:

■ How do you identify the slope and *y*-intercept from a linear equation?

■ Can you write and graph equations in slope-intercept form?

Directions

Read Question 1 and its solution. Then, write each equation in Questions 2 through 4 in slope-intercept form and identify the slope and *y*-intercept.

1. Write the equation $y + 2x = 1$ in slope-intercept form. Then identify the slope and *y*-intercept.

   Step 1   A linear equation in slope-intercept form is $y = mx + b$, where m is the slope of the line and b is the *y*-intercept. Solve for *y* to get $y = -2x + 1$.

   Step 2 $y = -2x + 1$, so the slope m is -2 and the *y*-intercept b is 1.

2. $y = -3x + 2$ 3. $y - 7 = 5x$ 4. $x = y + 3$

Use the problem scenario below to complete Questions 5 through 7.

Lindsay is a member of her high school cross-country team. She wants to reach the goal of running 500 miles over the summer. She has already run 220 miles and is running about 20 miles per week.

5. Write an equation that gives the total distance that Lindsay has run in terms of the number of weeks passed after the first 220 miles were completed.

6. Identify the slope and *y*-intercept of the equation in Question 5.

7. Draw a graph of the equation in Question 5 by using the slope and *y*-intercept.

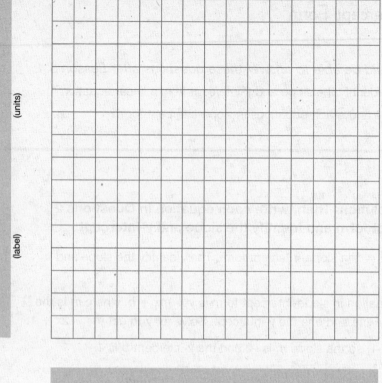

(units)

(label)

(label)   (units)

Saving Money

Writing Equations of Lines

Students should be able to answer these questions after Lesson 5.5:

- How are a point and slope used to write the equation of a line?
- How are two points used to write the equation of a line?

Directions

Read Question 1 and its solution. Then, in Questions 2 through 5, write an equation of the line that passes through the given point and has the given slope. Then write each equation in slope-intercept form.

1. Write an equation of the line that passes through (3, –1) and has a slope of 5. Then write the equation in slope-intercept form.

   Step 1

$y - y_1 = m(x - x_1)$	Point-slope form
$y - (-1) = 5(x - 3)$	Substitute 3 for x_1, –1 for y_1 and 5 for m.
$y + 1 = 5x - 15$	Simplify.

   Step 2 $y = 5x - 16$ Slope-intercept form

2. Passes through (–6, 0) and has slope –2

3. Passes through (9, 7) and has slope $\frac{1}{3}$

4. Passes through (–1, –8) and has slope 4

5. Passes through (2, –5) and has slope $-\frac{3}{2}$

Read Question 6 and its solution. Then, in Questions 7 through 10, write an equation of the line that passes through the given set of points. Then write each equation in slope-intercept form.

6. Write an equation of the line that passes through (–1, –3) and (2, 3). Then write the equation in slope-intercept form.

   Step 1   Find the slope of the line.

   $$m = \frac{y_2 - y_1}{x_2 - x_1} = \frac{3 - (-3)}{2 - (-1)} = \frac{6}{3} = 2$$

   Step 2

$y - y_1 = m(x - x_1)$	Point-slope form
$y - 3 = 2(x - 2)$	Substitute 2 for x_1, 3 for y_1 and 2 for m.
$y - 3 = 2x - 4$	Simplify.

   Step 3 $y = 2x - 1$ Slope-intercept form

7. Passes through (–6, 7) and (3, –11)

8. Passes through (2, –2) and (–4, –5)

9. Passes through (–4, 9) and (4, 3)

10. Passes through (–8, –34) and (–1, 8)

Spending Money
Linear and Piecewise Functions

Students should be able to answer these questions after Lesson 5.6:

■ Can you graph a piecewise function?

■ How are the equations for a piecewise function written?

Directions

Read the scenario below and complete Questions 1 through 8.

For many people, learning to use a credit card responsibly takes time. New credit card users are often surprised by how much they have spent when they receive their first bill.

Charlie recently opened his first credit card account. Although he vowed to spend responsibly, when he received the bill he was shocked to see that he had spent $500. He decided that he would not charge any more items until he has paid off his debt and maintained a zero balance for two months. He begins paying off his debt at a rate of $50 per month. After three months, he gets a raise at work and decides that he can increase his monthly payments to $75. Two months later he receives a bonus and decides to pay off the rest of his debt.

1. Complete the table below showing Charlie's debt.

Time since first bill	Debt
months	dollars
0	
1	
2	
3	
4	
5	
6	
7	

2. Use the grid on the next page to create a graph of the table in Question 1. First, choose your bounds and intervals.

Variable quantity	Lower bound	Upper bound	Interval
Time			
Debt			

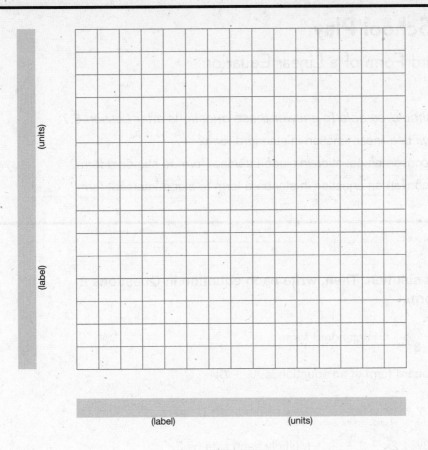

(units)

(label)

(label)   (units)

3. Write an equation that represents the piece of the function from 0 months to 3 months.

4. Write an equation that represents the piece of the function from 4 months to 5 months.

5. Write an equation that represents the piece of the function from 6 months to 8 months.

6. What is the domain of each piece of the function?

7. Use the equations from Questions 3, 4, and 5 and the domains from Question 6 to write a piecewise function.

8. What is the *y*-intercept of the graph? What does the *y*-intercept represent in this problem?

5

The School Play

Standard Form of a Linear Equation

Students should be able to answer these questions after Lesson 5.7:

- Can you write a linear function in standard form?
- Can you convert an equation in slope-intercept form to standard form?
- Can you convert an equation in standard form to slope-intercept form?

Directions

Read Question 1 and its solution. Then, write each equation in Questions 2 through 4 in standard form.

1. Write the equation $y = \dfrac{2}{3}x - 1$ in standard form.

   Step 1   The standard form of an equation is $Ax + By = C$.

   Step 2

   $$y = \dfrac{2}{3}x - 1$$

   $$3y = 2x - 3 \qquad \text{Multiply each side by 3.}$$

   $$-2x + 3y = -3 \qquad \text{Standard form}$$

2. $y = 3x - 12$ 3. $y = -\dfrac{1}{4}x + 6$ 4. $y = \dfrac{1}{2}x - 5$

Read Question 5 and its solution. Then, write each equation in Questions 6 through 8 in slope-intercept form.

5. Write the equation $4x + 8y = -6$ in slope-intercept form.

   Step 1   The slope-intercept form of an equation is $y = mx + b$

   Step 2 $4x + 8y = -6$

   $$8y = -4x - 6 \qquad \text{Isolate } y \text{ by subtracting } 4x \text{ from each side.}$$

   $$y = -\dfrac{1}{2}x - \dfrac{3}{4} \qquad \text{Divide each side by 8. Equation is in slope-intercept form.}$$

6. $-3x - y = 12$ 7. $x + 4y = -24$ 8. $-2x + 6y = 14$

Use the problem scenario below to complete Questions 9 through 11.

Tonight is opening night of the school play. Ticket prices are $4 for students and $5 for adults.

9. Write an expression that represents the total amount of money the drama club will raise from the sale of x student tickets and y adult tickets.

10. The drama club's goal is to raise $500 from opening night ticket sales. Write an equation in standard form that can be used to find the number of student and adult tickets sold to reach this goal.

11. Using the equation in Question 10, find the intercepts of the equation's graph. What do the intercepts mean in terms of the problem situation?

Earning Interest
Solving Literal Equations

Students should be able to answer these questions after Lesson 5.8:

■ What is a literal equation?

■ Can you solve a literal equation for a specified variable?

Directions

Read Question 1 and its solution. Then, complete Questions 2 through 5.

1. The formula for the volume of a rectangular prism is $V = lwh$ where V is the volume, l is the length, w is the width, and h is the height of the rectangular prism. Solve the equation for w. Then use a complete sentence to explain how you can find the width when you know the volume, length, and height of the rectangular prism.

   Step 1 $V = lwh$

   $$\frac{V}{lh} = w \qquad \text{Divide each side by } lh.$$

   Step 2   To find the width of a rectangular prism, divide the volume by the length and the height of the rectangular prism.

2. The formula for the circumference of a circle is $C = 2\pi r$ where C is the circumference, r is the radius, and the value of π is approximately 3.14. Solve the equation for r.

3. A hiker has been hiking for a week and will continue to hike for several more days. The formula for the total distance that he will hike is $D = d + rt$ where D is the total distance, d is the distance that he hiked the first week, r is his current rate, and t is the amount of time from now that he will hike. Solve the equation for t.

4. The formula for the sum of the interior angles of a polygon is $S = 180(n - 2)$ where S is the sum and n is the number of sides of the polygon. Solve the equation for n.

5. The formula for the area of a trapezoid is $A = \frac{1}{2}h(b_1 - b_2)$ where A is the area, h is the height of the trapezoid, and b_1 and b_2 are the lengths of the two bases of the trapezoid. Solve the equation for h.

6.1 Mia's Growing Like a Weed
Drawing the Line of Best Fit

Students should be able to answer these questions after Lesson 6.1:

■ Can you draw a line of best fit?

■ How is the equation of the line of best fit determined?

■ How is the line of best fit used to make predictions?

Directions

Use the problem scenario below to complete Questions 1 through 8.

Martha has been working as a paralegal for the same firm for the last 6 years. She would like to determine her potential future earnings to help decide whether to change careers.

Years with the law firm	Annual salary
years	dollars (in thousands)
0	20
1	21.2
2	23
3	23.5
4	25
5	26
6	28

1. Write ordered pairs from the table that shows Martha's salary as a function of the number of years with the law firm.

2. Create a scatter plot of the ordered pairs on the grid on the following page. First, choose your bounds and intervals.

Variable quantity	Lower bound	Upper bound	Interval
Years			
Salary			

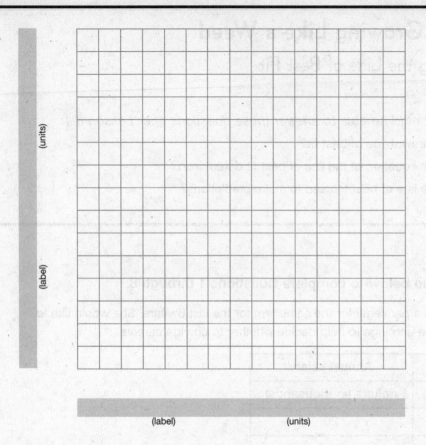

(units)

(label)

(label)   (units)

3. Use a ruler to draw the line that best fits the data on your graph.

Line of Best Fit

When drawing the line of best fit, try to get the same number of points above and below the line.

4. Write the equation of your line. Be sure to define your variables and include the units.

5. According to your line, approximately how much did Martha's salary increase each year during her 6 years at the law firm? How did you find your answer?

6. If Martha's salary continues to increase at this rate, how much will she be earning after 10 years at the law firm?

7. If Martha's salary continues to increase at this rate, how much will she be earning after 20 years at the law firm?

8. Do your answers to Questions 6 and 7 make sense? What can you conclude about the accuracy of your model?

6

6.2 Where Do You Buy Your Music?

Using Lines of Best Fit

Students should be able to answer these questions after Lesson 6.2:

- Can you use a line of best fit to make predictions?
- How are two lines of best fit compared?

Directions

Use the problem scenario below to complete Questions 1 through 7.

Martha has decided to consider the money that she will pay in taxes before deciding whether to accept a job offer that pays only slightly more. The table below shows her income and the amount that she paid in taxes.

Years with the law firm	Annual salary	Annual taxes paid
years	dollars (in thousands)	dollars (in thousands)
0	20	7.4
1	21.2	7.844
2	23	8.51
3	23.5	8.695
4	25	9.25
5	26	9.6
6	28	10.36

1. Write ordered pairs from the table that shows Martha's annual taxes as a function of the number of years with the law firm.

2. Create a scatter plot of the ordered pairs on the grid on the following page. First, choose your bounds and intervals.

Variable quantity	Lower bound	Upper bound	Interval
Years			
Taxes paid			

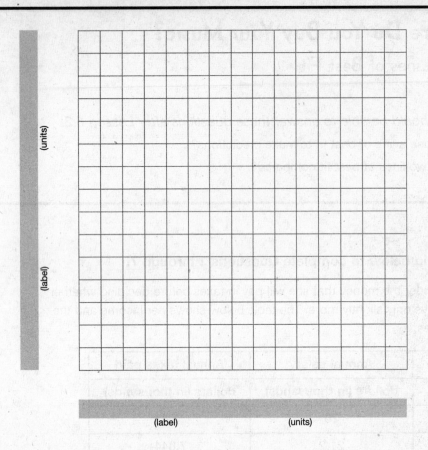

(units)

(label)

(label)   (units)

3. Use a ruler to draw the line that best fits the data on your graph. Then write the equation of the line. Define your variables and include units.

4. Use your equation to predict the amount Martha will pay in taxes after 10 years at the law firm.

5. Use your equation to predict the year in which Martha will pay $13,000 in taxes.

6. Do you think that the data from Homework Helper 6.1 and 6.2 are related? Use complete sentences in your answer.

7. Which line (if any) is increasing at a faster rate? Explain your answer.

6

6.3 Stroop Test
Performing an Experiment

Students should be able to answer these questions after Lesson 6.3:
- Can you perform an experiment?
- How is the line of best fit determined?
- Can you analyze the results of an experiment?

Directions

Perform the experiment below. Then, use the results from your experiment to complete Questions 1 through 11.

The Stroop Test studies a person's perception of words and colors. A person that participates in the Stroop Test will receive one of two lists, a matching list or a non-matching list with a varying number of words. In a matching list, the color of the ink matches the color of the word. In a non-matching list, the color of the ink does not match the color of the word. Use the steps below to perform the Stroop Test with a partner.

Step 1 Using the color words red, green, black, and blue, make several lists of varying length in which the ink and the color words match. For instance, write the word "red" in red ink.

Step 2 Using the color words red, green, black, and blue, make several lists of varying length in which the ink and the color words do not match. For instance, write the word "red" in black ink.

Step 3 Give your partner either kind of list. Have him or her say aloud the color of the ink in which each word in the list is written. Record the time in takes to finish saying the list aloud.

Step 4 Record your data in the table below.

Matching Lists		Non-matching Lists	
List length (words)	Time (seconds)	List length (words)	Time (seconds)

1. Write the ordered pairs from the matching lists table that show the time as a function of the length of the list.

2. Create a scatter plot of the ordered pairs on the grid below. First, choose your bounds and intervals.

Variable quantity	Lower bound	Upper bound	Interval
List length			
Time			

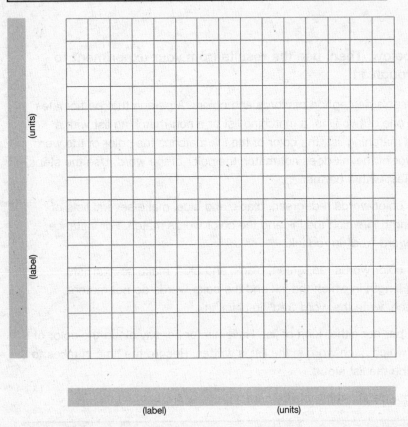

(units)

(label)

(label)   (units)

3. Use a ruler to draw the line of best fit. Then write the equation of your line.

4. How many seconds should it take a person to say the color of the ink of a matching list of 30 words?

5. Of how many words should a person be able to say the color of the ink from a matching list in 3 minutes?

6. Write the ordered pairs from the non-matching lists table that shows the time as a function of the length of the list.

6

7. Create a scatter plot of the ordered pairs on the grid below. First, choose your bounds and intervals.

Variable quantity	Lower bound	Upper bound	Interval
List length			
Time			

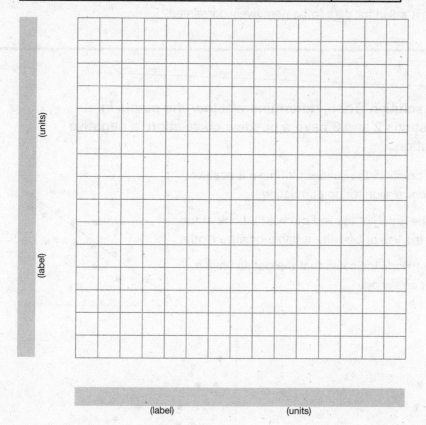

(units)

(label)

(label)   (units)

8. Use a ruler to draw the line of best fit. Then write the equation of your line.

9. How many seconds should it take a person to say the color of the ink of a non-matching list of 30 words?

10. Of how many words should a person be able to say the color of the ink for from a non-matching list in 3 minutes?

11. Compare your results for the matching lists to the results for the non-matching lists. Do your results seem reasonable?

6

Jumping

Correlation

Students should be able to answer these questions after Lesson 6.4:

■ What does it mean for data to be positively correlated?

■ What does it mean for data to be negatively correlated?

Directions

Read Question 1 and its solution. Then, determine whether the points in each scatter plot in Questions 2 and 3 have a positive correlation, a negative correlation, or no correlation.

1. Determine whether the points in the scatter plot have a positive correlation, a negative correlation, or no correlation.

    Step 1 Sketch the grpah of the line of best fit. Look at the slope of the line of best fit. It has a positive slope.

    Step 2 A positive slope indicates that the points have a positive correlation.

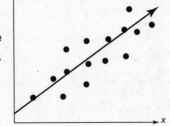

2.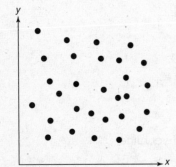

3.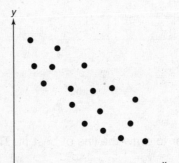

Read Question 4 and its solution. Then, decide whether each data set described in Questions 5 through 7 would have a positive correlation, negative correlation, or no correlation.

4. Is the time you spent practicing the piano and the number of mistakes you make at the recital positively correlated, negatively correlated, or not correlated?

    Step 1 As the time you spend practicing increases, you would expect to master your skills, resulting in less mistakes. So, this data would have a negative correlation.

5. Time spent driving and distance traveled

6. Amount of money spent and the amount in your savings account

7. The year and the amount of rainfall in Cleveland, OH

6.5 Human Chain: Wrist Experiment
Using Technology to Find a Linear Regression Equation, Part I

Students should be able to answer these questions after Lesson 6.5:

■ How do you use a calculator to generate a linear regression equation?

■ What does the *r*-value tell you about the data?

Directions

Use the data points below to complete Questions 1 through 11.

(3, –2), (5, 1), (6, 11), (7, 16), (10, 30), (12, 35), (15, 40), (17, 47), (9, 20)

1. To find the linear regression equation for a set of data, you must first enter the data into the calculator. Enter the *x*-values into one list and the *y*-values into another list.

2. After the data have been entered, use the linear regression feature of your calculator to find the linear regression. Most calculators display the slope, usually denoted by *a*, and the *y*-intercept, usually denoted by *b*, along with a value for the correlation coefficient, usually denoted by *R*.

3. The value of *a* is the slope of the line. What is the slope of the line to the nearest hundredth?

4. The value of *b* is the *y*-intercept. What is the *y*-intercept to the nearest tenth?

5. Write the equation of the line of best fit in slope-intercept form.

6. What is the value of *r* for your linear regression equation? Does this value indicate a positive or negative correlation? How do you know?

7. How close are your data to being a straight line? Use a complete sentence in your explanation.

8. Use your regression equation to determine the value of *y* when *x* is 25.

9. Use your regression equation to determine the value of *y* when *x* is –10.

10. Use your regression equation to determine the value of *x* when *y* is 43.

11. Use your regression equation to determine the value of *x* when *y* is –18.

6

Human Chain: Shoulder Experiment

Using Technology to Find a Linear Regression Equation, Part 2

Students should be able to answer these questions after Lesson 6.6:

■ How do you use a calculator to generate a linear regression equation?

■ How is the linear regression equation used to make predictions?

Directions

The table below shows the number of male participants in high school athletic programs from 1995–96 to 2003–04. Use the table to complete Questions 1 through 10.

Year	1995	1996	1997	1998	1999	2000	2001	2002	2003
Male participants (in millions)	3.63	3.71	3.76	3.83	3.86	3.92	3.96	3.99	4.04

1. Write the ordered pairs from the table that show the number of male participants as a function of the year.

2. Because the *x*-coordinates represent time, we can define time as the number of years since 1995. So, 1995 becomes 0, 1996 becomes 1, and so on. Now write the ordered pairs that show the number of participants as a function of the number of years since 1995.

3. Create a scatter plot of the ordered pairs on the grid on the following page. The bounds and intervals are chosen for you. Because the data is clustered together, break the graph to show the portion where the data appears.

Variable quantity	Lower bound	Upper bound	Interval
Year	0	15	1
Male participants	3.5	4.48	0.07

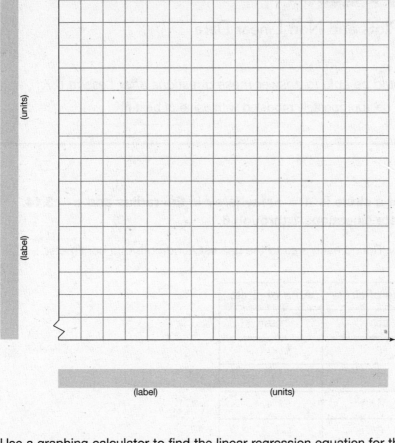

(units)

(label)

(label)   (units)

4. Use a graphing calculator to find the linear regression equation for the data. Then graph the line on the grid above.

5. How close are the data to forming a straight line? Use a complete sentence to explain your reasoning.

6. What is the slope of the linear regression equation? What does the slope mean in the problem situation?

7. Use your linear regression equation to predict the number of male participants in 2005.

8. Use your linear regression equation to predict the number of male participants in 2010.

9. Use your linear regression equation to determine in what year there will be about 4.5 million male participants in high school athletic programs.

10. Use your linear regression equation to determine in what year there were about 3.2 million male participants in high school athletic programs.

6.7 Making a Quilt

Scatter Plots and Non-Linear Data

Students should be able to answer these questions after Lesson 6.7:

■ Can all data be appropriately modeled with a line of best fit?

Directions

The formula for the area of a circle is $A = \pi r^2$ where r is the radius and $\pi \approx 3.14$. Use the formula to complete Questions 1 through 6.

1. Complete the table below. Round each area to the nearest hundredth of a centimeter.

Labels	Radius of circle	Area of circle
Units	cm	cm²
Expressions	r	πr^2
	2	
	4	
	6	
	8	
	10	

2. Write the ordered pairs that show the area as a function of the radius.

3. Create a scatter plot of the ordered pairs on the grid on the following page. First, choose your bounds and intervals.

Variable quantity	Lower bound	Upper bound	Interval
Radius of circle			
Area of circle			

6

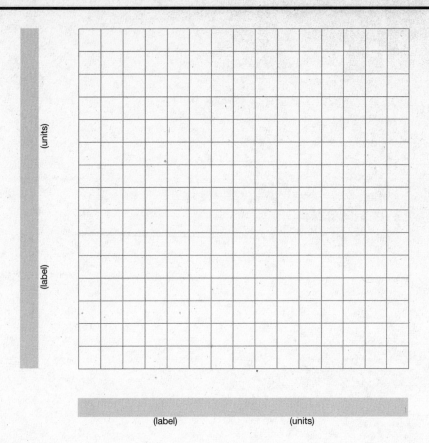

(units)

(label)

(label)   (units)

4. Use a ruler to draw a line of best fit on the graph in Question 3. Then write the equation of your line.

5. Use a complete sentence to describe the shape of the graph of the data in Question 3.

6. Use the area formula to find the area of a circle with a radius of 20 centimeters. Then use the equation you wrote in Question 4 to find the area. What can you conclude about making a prediction with your linear model?

6

7.1 Making and Selling Markers and T-Shirts
Using a Graph to Solve a Linear System

Students should be able to answer these questions after Lesson 7.1:

- What does the break-even point tell you?
- How do you find the break-even point?

Directions

Read Question 1 and its solution. Then, use the scenario to complete Questions 2 through 8.

1. Maggie is making and selling knitted scarves to make extra money. It costs her $12 for yarn to make one scarf and $30 for an assortment of knitting needles. Maggie will sell the scarves for $15 per scarf. Write an equation that gives Maggie's production cost in terms of the number of scarves made. Then write an equation that gives Maggie's income in terms of the number of scarves sold.

   Step 1 Maggie's production cost can be represented by the equation $y = 12x + 30$ where x is the number of scarves produced and y is the production cost in dollars.

   Step 2 Maggie's income can be represented by the equation $y = 15x$ where x is the number of scarves sold and y is the income in dollars.

2. Complete the table of values that shows the production cost and income for different numbers of scarves.

Labels	Number of scarves	Product costs	Income
Units	scarves	dollars	dollars
Expressions	x		
	0		
	5		
	10		
	15		
	20		

3. Profit is the amount of money that is left from sales after the production costs are subtracted. What is Maggie's profit if she makes and sells 10 scarves? What is Maggie's profit if she makes and sells 20 scarves? Use complete sentences in your answers.

Break-Even Point

The break-even point is the point at which production costs are equal to income. At this point, the profit equals zero,

4. According to your table and your calculations, what is the break-even point? Use complete sentences to explain your answer.

5. Create a graph of both the production costs and income equations on the grid below. Use the bounds and intervals below. Be sure to label your graph clearly.

Variable quantity	Lower bound	Upper bound	Interval
Scarves	0	30	2
Money	0	300	20

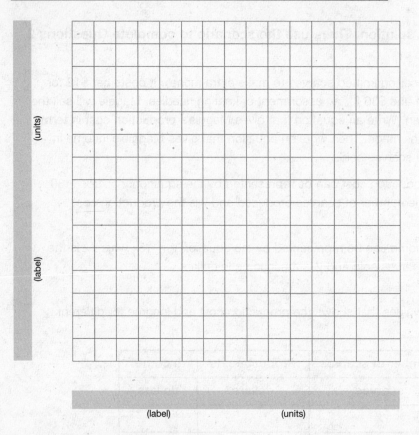

(units)

(label)

(label)   (units)

6. Use your graph to determine the numbers of scarves for which the production cost is greater than the income.

7. Use your graph to determine the numbers of scarves for which the income is greater than the production cost.

8. Use your graph to determine the number of scarves for which the income is equal to the production cost. What is this point called?

Time Study

Graphs and Solutions of Linear Systems

Students should be able to answer these questions after Lesson 7.2:

- How many solutions can a linear system have?
- How does the graph of a linear system relate to the solution?
- What are the characteristics of parallel and perpendicular lines??

Directions

Read Question 1 and its solution. Then, determine whether each system in Questions 2 through 4 has one solution, no solution, or an infinite number of solutions. Use a complete sentence to justify your answer.

1. Determine whether the linear system $y = 3x - 4$ and $y = 5 + 3x$ has one solution, no solution, or an infinite number of solutions.

   Step 1 Look at the slope of each line.

   $y = 3x - 4$ has a slope of 3. $y = 5 + 3x$ also has a slope of 3.

   Step 2 Because the slopes are equal, look at the y-intercepts. If the y-intercepts are different, then the lines are parallel (no solution). If the y-intercepts are the same, then the lines have the same graph (infinite solutions). The y-intercepts in this system are different, so the lines are parallel and the linear system has no solution.

2. $y = -5x + 6$

   $y = 4x - 10$

3. $y = 2(x + 7)$

   $y = 2x + 14$

4. $y = 8x - 12$

   $y = 4(2x + 3)$

Read Question 5 and its solution. Then, determine whether the graphs of each pair of equations in Questions 6 through 8 are parallel, perpendicular, or neither.

5. Determine whether the graphs of the equations $y = 4x - 7$ and $y = -\frac{1}{4}x + 3$ are parallel, perpendicular, or neither.

   Step 1 Look at the slope of each line.

   $y = 4x - 7$ has a slope of 4. $y = -\frac{1}{4}x + 3$ has a slope of $-\frac{1}{4}$.

   Step 2 Find the product of the slopes.

   $4\left(-\frac{1}{4}\right) = -1$ The lines are perpendicular because the product of the slopes is –1.

6. $y = 2x - 4$

$y = 2x + 9$

7. $y = \dfrac{1}{3}x + 5$

$y = 3x + 6$

8. $y = \dfrac{2}{3}x + 1$

$y = -\dfrac{6}{4}x - 8$

7.3 Hiking Trip

Using Substitution to Solve a Linear System

Students should be able to answer this question after Lesson 7.3:

■ Can you solve a linear system by using substitution?

Directions

Read Question 1 and its solution. Then solve each linear system in Questions 2 through 4 by using the substitution method.

1. Solve the linear system by using the substitution method.

   $4x - 2y = -26$

   $y = 4 - x$

   Step 1 Substitute $4 - x$ for y in the first equation and solve for x.

   $$4x - 2y = -26$$

   $$4x - 2(4 - x) = -26$$

   $$4x - 8 + 2x = -26$$

   $$6x = -18$$

   $$x = -3$$

   Step 2 Substitute -3 for x into the equation $y = 4 - x$ to find y.

   $$y = 4 - x = 4 - (-3) = 7$$

   The solution is $(-3, 7)$.

2. $-3x - y = -14$

   $y = 4x$

3. $2x - 5y = -23$

   $3x + y = -9$

4. $6x - 5y = 0$

   $4x + 10y = -28$

5. Cindy is taking a painting class. She spent $57 on supplies at the art supply store. Each paintbrush cost $2.50 and each tube of oil paint cost $5.50. Cindy bought one paint brush for every three tubes of paint. Write a system of linear equations that represents this situation. Use x to represent the number of paintbrushes and y to represent the number of tubes of paint. Will 4 paintbrushes and 12 tubes of paint satisfy both of your equations? Use substitution to solve the linear system. Interpret your solution.

7.4 Basketball Tournament
Using Linear Combinations to Solve a Linear System

Students should be able to answer this question after Lesson 7.4:

■ How do you solve a system of equations using linear combinations?

Directions

Read Question 1 and its solution. Then solve each linear system in Questions 2 through 4 by using linear combinations.

1. Solve the linear system by using linear combinations.

   $3x - 4y = 7$

   $2x - y = 3$

   Step 1   Multiply the second equation by −4 to get the coefficients of y to be opposites.

   $-4(2x - y) = -4(3)$

   $-8x + 4y = -12$

   Step 2   Write new system. Then add the equations.

   $3x - 4y = 7$

   $-8x + 4y = -12$
   _____

   $-5x = -5$

   $x = 1$

   Step 3   Substitute the value of x into the second equation to find y.

   $2(1) - y = 3$

   $y = -1$

   The solution is (1, −1).

2. $x + 4y = 23$

   $-x + y = 2$

3. $x + y = 1$

   $2y - x = 2$

4. $3x + 5y = 6$

   $-4x + 2y = 5$

5. A local animal shelter helps place dogs and cats with families. While in the shelter, dogs are kept in kennels by themselves, while cats are kept two per kennel. The shelter has 200 kennels in which to keep dogs and cats awaiting adoption. The shelter currently has 300 animals. Write a system of linear equations that represents this situation. Use x to represent the number of dogs and y to represent the number of cats. Use linear combinations to solve the linear system. Interpret your solution.

7.5 Finding the Better Paying Job
Using the Best Method to Solve a Linear System, Part 1

Students should be able to answer this question after Lesson 7.5:

■ How do you identify the best algebraic method to solve a linear system?

Directions

Read Question 1 and its solution. Then, solve each system of linear equations in Questions 2 through 5. Tell which method you used to solve each system and explain your choice.

1. Solve the following system of linear equations. Which method did you use to find the answer? Use a complete sentence to explain your choice.

$$x - 2y = -8$$
$$-2x - 4y = -56$$

Step 1 Both equations are in standard form, so we will use linear combinations to solve this linear system. If one or both equations were in slope-intercept form, we would use substitution to solve the system.

Step 2 Multiply the first equation by 2 to get the coefficients of x to be opposites.

$$2(x - 2y) = 2(-8)$$
$$2x - 4y = -16$$

Step 3 Write the new system and add the equations.

$$2x - 4y = -16$$
$$\underline{-2x - 4y = -56}$$
$$-8y = -72$$
$$y = 9$$

Step 4 Substitute the value of y into the first equation to find x.

$$x - 2(9) = -8$$
$$x = 10$$

The solution is (10, 9).

2. $5y + 3x = 10$

   $y = -2x + 2$

3. $2x - y = 14$

   $-x - y = 2$

4. $4x + y = -11$

   $-3x + 2y = -11$

5. $-x - 5y = -37$

   $y + 2x = 2$

World Oil: Supply and Demand

Using the Best Method to Solve a Linear System, Part 2

7

Students should be able to answer this question after Lesson 7.6:

- How do you identify the best algebraic method to solve a linear system?

Directions

Read Question 1 and its solution. Then, use the scenario to answer Questions 2 through 9.

1. The projected national supply and demand of registered nurses for 2000 and 2010 are shown in the table. Write an equation that gives the supply of nurses in millions in terms of the number of years since 2000. Assume that the rate of change in the supply is the same as the rate of change from 2000 to 2010.

	Supply of RNs (in millions)	Demand of RNs (in millions)
2000	1.89	2.00
2010	2.07	2.34

Step 1 Find the rate of change.

$$\frac{2.07 - 1.89}{2010 - 2000} = \frac{0.18}{10} = 0.018$$

Step 2 Let x represent the number of years since 2000 and let y represent the supply in millions of nurses. Then the graph of the equation passes through the point (0, 1.89) and has a slope of 0.018. The equation is $y = 0.018x + 1.89$.

2. Use the scenario in Question 1 to write an equation that gives the demand of nurses in millions in terms of the number of years since 2000. Assume that the rate of change in the demand is the same as the rate of change from 2000 to 2010.

3. In which year will the supply be 2.25 million registered nurses?

4. Find the demand in 2013.

5. In which year will the demand be 2.5 million registered nurses?

6. Find the supply 3 years before 2000.

7. Write the linear system that represents the supply and the demand since 2003.

8. Solve the linear system in Question 7 to determine when the supply and the demand were equal. Which method did you use to find your answer?

9. How many registered nurses were there when the supply and demand were equal?

7.7   Picking the Better Option

Solving Linear Systems

Students should be able to answer this question after Lesson 7.7:

■ What are the different methods of solving linear systems?

Directions

Use the scenario below to complete Questions 1 through 7.

A car manufacturer is considering two new fuel-efficient vehicles to introduce next fall. The production costs for the first model, the EcoRide, will be $275,000 to develop the prototype and $7500 for each vehicle manufactured. The production costs for the second model, the Green Machine, will be $245,000 to develop the prototype and $10,000 for each vehicle manufactured.

1. For each model, write an equation that gives the total cost in dollars in terms of the number of vehicles manufactured. Be sure to define your variables.

2. For each model, what do the slope and *y*-intercept of the graph of the equation represent in the problem situation?

3. Will there be a number of vehicles for which the total costs are the same? How do you know? Use complete sentences to explain your reasoning.

4. Use an algebraic method to find the number of vehicles for which the total costs are the same. Then describe the numbers of vehicles for which each model is less expensive.

5. The automobile manufacturer plans to sell the fuel-efficient vehicle for $28,000 each. Write an equation that gives the total earnings in dollars in terms of the number of vehicles sold.

6. For each model, determine the break-even point. Recall that the break-even point is the *x*-coordinate of the point where the graph of the cost intersects the graph of the income.

7. Use the results from Question 4 and Question 6 to describe the numbers of vehicles for which each model is better.

7.8 Video Arcade

Writing and Graphing an Inequality in Two Variables

Students should be able to answer these questions after Lesson 7.8:

■ How does the graph of a linear inequality differ from the graph of a linear equation?

■ How do you graph a linear inequality?

Directions

Read Question 1 and its solution. Then graph each linear inequality in Questions 2 and 3.

1. Graph the linear inequality $y \leq 2x - 1$.

    Step 1 Graph the line $y \leq 2x - 1$. Because the inequality symbol is $\leq$, the line is included in the graph, and so is represented by a solid line.

    Step 2 Test a point and shade the half plane. Select any point that is not on the line and substitute the x and y values into the inequality. Test the point $(0, 0)$.

    $$0 \overset{?}{\leq} 2(0) - 1$$

    $$0 \leq -1$$

    The point $(0, 0)$ does not satisfy the inequality, so shade the half-plane that does not contain $(0, 0)$.

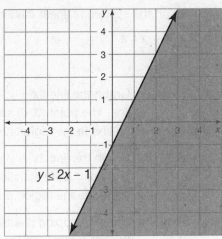

2. $y > 3x + 2$

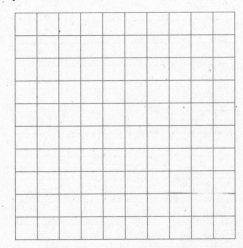

3. $y \geq -2x - 3$

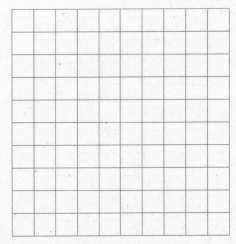

7.9 Making a Mosaic
Solving Systems of Linear Inequalities

Students should be able to answer these questions after Lesson 7.9:

■ How do you graph a system of linear inequalities?

■ What does the solution of a system of linear inequalities look like?

Directions

Read Question 1 and its solution. Then graph each system of linear inequalities in Questions 2 and 3.

1. Graph the system of linear inequalities.

   $2x + y \geq -4$

   $x - 2y < 4$

   Step 1 Graph the line $2x + y = -4$. Use a solid line. The point $(0, 0)$ satisfies the inequality, so shade the region above the line.

   Step 2 Graph the line $2x + y = -4$. Use a dashed line. The point $(0, 0)$ satisfies the inequality, so shade the region above the line.

   Step 3 The overlapping shaded region is the solution of the linear inequalities.

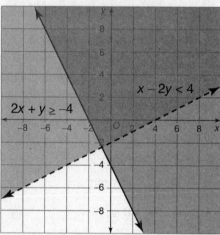

2. $3x + y < 15$

   $-2x - 2y \geq -8$

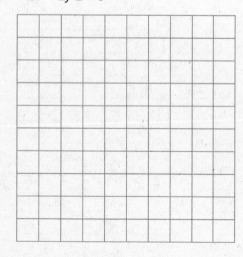

3. $-x + y \leq 3$

   $-x + y > -3$

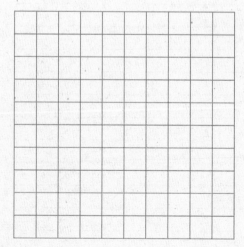

8.1 Website Design

Introduction to Quadratic Functions

Students should be able to answer these questions after Lesson 8.1:

- Can you identify the coefficients in a quadratic function?
- What does the graph of a quadratic function look like?

Directions

Read Question 1 and its solution. Then, identify the values of *a*, *b*, and *c* in each quadratic function in Questions 2 through 5.

1. Identify the values of a, b, and c in the quadratic function $y = x - 2x^2 - 6$.

   Step 1   Rewrite the function in standard form, $y = ax^2 + bx + c$.

   $$y = x - 2x^2 - 6 = -2x^2 + x - 6 = (-2)x^2 + x + (-6)$$

   Step 2   Identify a, b, and c: $a = -2$, $b = 1$, and $c = -6$.

2. $y = -x^2 - 4x$

3. $y = x^2 - 8$

4. $y = -10 + x^2 + 9x$

5. $y = 20 - \dfrac{1}{2}x^2$

Read Question 6 and its solution. Then, evaluate each quadratic function in Questions 7 through 10 for the given value of the variable.

6. Evaluate $f(x) = 3x^2 + 4x - 10$ for $x = -2$.

   Step 1   Substitute –2 for x.

   Step 2   Simplify. Follow the order of operations.

   $$f(-2) = 3(-2)^2 + 4(-2) - 10$$
   $$= 3(4) + 4(-2) - 10$$
   $$= 12 - 8 - 10$$
   $$= -6$$

7. $g(x) = x^2 + 3x + 5$; $g(3)$

8. $h(x) = -4x^2 - 3x + 8$; $h(-1)$

9. $f(x) = 6x^2 + 10$; $f(8)$

10. $g(x) = -19 - 3x^2$; $g(-2)$

11. Complete the table below for the function . Then use the values in the table to create a graph of the function on the grid below.

x	$x^2 + 4x - 2$
–4	
–3	
–2	
–1	
0	
1	
2	

Note

The graph of a quadratic equation (called a parabola) is a U-shaped graph.

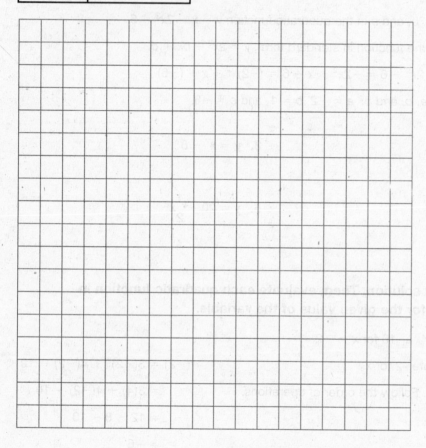

8.2 Satellite Dish
Parabolas

Students should be able to answer these questions after Lesson 8.2:

- Can you find the line of symmetry of a parabola?
- What is the vertex of a parabola and how do you find it?
- Can you identify the maximum or minimum value of a quadratic function?

Directions

Read Question 1 and its solution. Then, for each quadratic function in Questions 2 and 3, (a) complete the table of values, (b) create a graph of the function, (c) find the line of symmetry, and (d) find the vertex.

1. Create a graph of the function $y = x^2 + 3x - 4$. Then find the line of symmetry and the vertex of the function.

   Step 1   Use the table of values to create a graph of the function.

x	$x^2 + 3x - 4$
–2	$(-2)^2 + 3(-2) - 4 = -6$
–1	$(-1)^2 + 3(-1) - 4 = -6$
0	$(0)^2 + 3(0) - 4 = -4$
1	$(1)^2 + 3(1) - 4 = 0$
2	$(2)^2 + 3(2) - 4 = 6$

   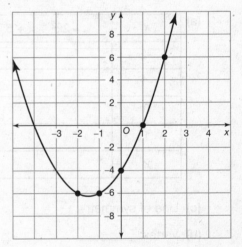

   Step 2   Find the line of symmetry.

   $$x = \frac{b}{2a} = -\frac{3}{2(1)} = -\frac{3}{2}$$

   Step 3   Find the vertex.

   The x-coordinate is on the line of symmetry.

   So, $x = -\frac{3}{2}$.

   The y-coordinate is $y = \left(-\frac{3}{2}\right)^2 + 3\left(-\frac{3}{2}\right) - 4 = \frac{9}{4} - \frac{9}{2} - 4 = -\frac{25}{4}$.

   The vertex is $\left(-\frac{3}{2}, -\frac{25}{4}\right)$.

   The y-coordinate of the vertex, $-\frac{25}{4}$, is the minimum of the function.

2. $y = x^2 + 2x + 5$

(a)

x	$x^2 + 2x + 5$
−2	
−1	
0	
1	
2	

(b)

(c) Line of symmetry: _____

(d) Vertex: _____

Is the y-coordinate of the vertex a minimum or maximum?

3. $y = x^2 + 2x + 5$

(a)

x	$-2x^2 + x + 5$
−2	
−1	
0	
1	
2	

(b)

(c) Line of symmetry: _____

(d) Vertex: _____

Is the y-coordinate of the vertex a minimum or maximum?

Dog Run

Comparing Linear and Quadratic Functions

Students should be able to answer these questions after Lesson 8.3:

■ How does the graph of a quadratic function compare to the graph of a linear function?

■ Can you use linear and quadratic functions to model a situation?

Directions

Complete Questions 1 through 8.

1. A rectangle has a width of *x* meters. The perimeter of the rectangle is 18 meters. Complete the table below to show different widths, lengths, and areas that can occur with this restriction.

Width	Length	Area
meters	meters	square meters
0		
2		
4		
6		
8		

2. Create a graph that shows the length as a function of the width on the grid on the next page. First, choose your bounds and intervals.

Variable quantity	Lower bound	Upper bound	Interval
Width			
Area			

(units)

(label)

(label)   (units)

3. What kind of function is represented by the graph in Question 2? How do you know? Use a complete sentence in your answer.

4. Create a graph that shows the area as a function of the width on the grid on the next page. First, choose your bounds and intervals.

Variable quantity	Lower bound	Upper bound	Interval
Width			
Area			

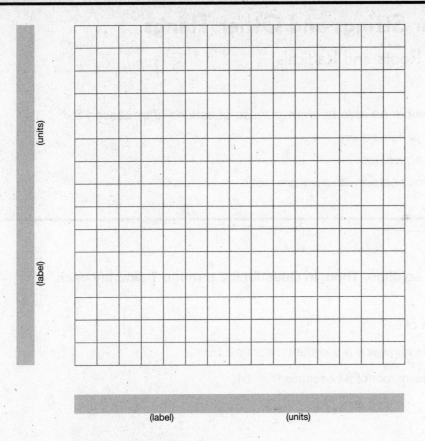

(units)

(label)

(label)   (units)

5. What kind of function is represented by the graph in Question 4? How do you know? Use a complete sentence in your answer.

6. What are the *x*- and *y*-intercepts of the graph of the linear function? What is their meaning in the problem situation? Use complete sentences in your answer.

7. What are the *x*- and *y*-intercepts of the graph of the quadratic function? What is their meaning in the problem situation? Use complete sentences in your answer.

8. What is the greatest possible area? What are the length and width of the rectangle with the greatest possible area? Use complete sentences to explain how you found your answer.

8.4 Guitar Strings and Other Things

Square Roots and Radicals

Students should be able to answer these questions after Lesson 8.4:

- What is a perfect square?
- What is a square root?
- How do you approximate a square root?

Directions

Read Question 1 and its solution. Then, in Questions 2 through 7 simplify each square root.

1. What is the square root of 64?

   Step 1   A positive number b is a square root of a if $b^2 = a$.

   Step 2   8 is a square root of 64 because $8^2 = 64$.

2. $\sqrt{1}$

3. $\sqrt{16}$

4. $-\sqrt{144}$

5. $-\sqrt{9}$

6. $\sqrt{121}$

7. $-\sqrt{49}$

Read Question 8 and its solution. Then, in Questions 9 through 14 approximate each square root to the nearest tenth.

8. Approximate $\sqrt{32}$ to the nearest tenth.

   Step 1   Find the perfect squares closest to 32.

   The perfect square that is closest to 32 and is less than 32 is 25.

   The perfect square that is closest to 32 and is greater than 32 is 36.

   Step 2   32 is between 25 and 36 and $\sqrt{32}$ is between $\sqrt{25} = 5$ and $\sqrt{36} = 6$.

   Step 3   Estimate $\sqrt{32}$ by choosing numbers between 5 and 6. Test each number by finding its square and seeing how close it is to 32.

   $5.6^2 = 31.36$ $5.7^2 = 32.49$

   So, $\sqrt{32} \approx 5.7$.

9. $\sqrt{23}$

10. $\sqrt{92}$

11. $\sqrt{67}$

12. $\sqrt{80}$

13. $\sqrt{41}$

14. $\sqrt{11}$

Tent Designing Competition
Solving by Factoring and Extracting Square Roots

Students should be able to answer these questions after Lesson 8.5:

- How is a quadratic equation solved by factoring?
- How does the solution of a quadratic equation relate to the *x*-intercepts?

Directions

Read Question 1 and its solution. Then, find the *x*- and *y*-intercepts of the graph of each factored quadratic equation in Questions 2 through 4.

1. Consider the equation $y = 2(x - 3)(x + 3)$. Algebraically find the *x*- and *y*-intercepts of the graph.

   Step 1   To find the *x*-intercepts, substitute 0 for *y* and solve for *x*.

   $$0 = 2(x - 3)(x + 3)$$

   When one of the factors in the equation is zero, then the product is zero. So, set each factor equal to zero and solve for *x*.

   $x - 3 = 0$ $\qquad\qquad$ $x + 3 = 0$

   $\quad x = 3$ $\qquad\qquad\quad$ $x = -3$

   The *x*-intercepts are 3 and –3.

   Step 2   To find the *y*-intercept, substitute 0 for *x* and solve for *y*.

   $$y = 2(0 - 3)(0 + 3) = 2(-3)(3) = -18$$

   The *y*-intercept is –18.

2. $y = \dfrac{1}{4}(x - 1)(x + 1)$ $\qquad$ 3. $y = -(x + 3)(x + 1)$ $\qquad$ 4. $y = -5(x - 3)(x - 2)$

Read Question 5 and its solution. Then, solve each equation in Questions 6 through 8. Approximate your answers to the nearest tenth, if necessary.

5. Solve $4x^2 - 100 = 0$.

    Step 1   Isolate the variable on one side of the equation.

$$4x^2 - 100 = 0$$
$$4x^2 = 100$$
$$x^2 = 25$$

    Step 2   Solve for x by finding the square roots of 25.

$$x = 5 \text{ and } x = -5$$

6. $x^2 + 9 = 58$ 7. $3x^2 = 18$ 8. $7x^2 - 11 = 52$

Kicking a Soccer Ball

Using the Quadratic Formula to Solve Quadratic Equations

Students should be able to answer these questions after Lesson 8.6:

■ What is the Quadratic Formula?

■ How do you determine the number of solutions that a quadratic function has?

Directions

Read Question 1 and its solution. Then, use the Quadratic Formula to solve each equation in Questions 2 through 4.

1. Use the Quadratic Formula to find the solutions of the equation $x^2 - 4x = 5$.

   Step 1   To use the Quadratic Formula, the equation must be in the form $ax^2 + bx + c = 0$. So, set the equation equal to zero.

   $x^2 - 4x - 5 = 0$ Subtract 5 from each side.

   Step 2   Identify the values of a, b, and c.

   $a = 1$, $b = -4$, and $c = -5$

   Step 3   Substitute the values of a, b, and c into the Quadratic Formula and simplify.

   $$x = \frac{-b \pm \sqrt{b^2 - 4ac}}{2a}$$

   $$= \frac{-(-4) \pm \sqrt{(-4)^2 - 4(1)(-5)}}{2(1)}$$

   $$= \frac{4 \pm \sqrt{36}}{2}$$

   $$= \frac{4 \pm 6}{2}$$

   $$= \frac{10}{2} = 5; \text{ and } \frac{-2}{2} = -1$$

2. $2x^2 + 3x = 5$

3. $x - 14 = -4x^2$

4. $10x^2 + 31x + 24 = 0$

Read Question 5 and its solution. Then, tell if each equation in Questions 6 through 8 has one solution, two solutions, or no solution.

5. How many solutions does the equation $-x^2 + 2x - 1 = 0$ have?

> **Step 1**   Find the value of the discriminant.
>
> $b^2 - 4ac = (2)^2 - 4(-1)(-1) = 4 - 4 = 0$
>
> **Step 2**   The discriminant is zero, so the equation has one solution.

> ### Discriminant
>
> If $b^2 - 4ac > 0$, then the equation has two solutions.
>
> If $b^2 - 4ac = 0$, then the equation has one solution.
>
> If $b^2 - 4ac < 0$, then the equation has no real solution.

6. $3x^2 + 4x - 1 = 0$

7. $-4x^2 - 8x - 4 = 0$

8. $5x^2 - 6x + 2 = 0$

8.7 Pumpkin Catapult
Using a Vertical Motion Model

Students should be able to answer this question after Lesson 8.7:

■ How are quadratic equations used to model vertical motion?

8

Directions

Read Question 1 and its solution. Then, use the problem scenario to complete Questions 2 through 7.

1. Marcus is playing lacrosse. He throws the ball upward from his playing stick at an initial height of 7 feet and with an initial velocity of 90 feet per second. Write a quadratic function that models the height of the ball in terms of time.

   Step 1   The vertical motion model is $y = -16t^2 + vt + h$, where t is the time that the ball has been moving in seconds, v is the initial velocity of the ball in feet per second, h is the initial height of the ball in feet, and y is the height of the ball in feet at time t seconds.

   Step 2   In the problem scenario, $v = 90$ and $h = 7$. Substitute these values to get the equation $y = -16t^2 + 90t + 7$.

2. Write an equation that you can use to determine when the ball will hit the ground. Then solve the equation. Show all your work.

3. Do both solutions have meaning in the problem situation? Use a complete sentence to explain your reasoning.

4. What is the height of the ball 3 seconds after Marcus throws the ball from his playing stick?

5. When is the ball at its highest point? Show all your work and use a complete sentence in your answer.

6. What is the greatest height of the ball? Use a complete sentence in your answer.

7. When is the ball at a height of 115 feet? Use a complete sentence in your answer.

8.8 Viewing the Night Sky
Using Quadratic Functions

Students should be able to answer these questions after Lesson 8.8:

■ How are quadratic functions used to model the shape of an object?

■ How do the vertex, axis of symmetry, domain, and range relate to the graph of a quadratic function?

Directions

Read Question 1 and its solution. Then, use the graph of the function to complete Questions 2 through 8.

1. Graph the functions $y = \frac{1}{4}x^2$, $y = -2x^2$, and $y = 4x^2$ on the same grid on the next page.

Use the bounds and intervals given below.

Variable quantity	Lower bound	Upper bound	Interval
x	9	9	1
y	120	150	15

Step 1 Use a table of values to help you graph each function.

x	$y = \frac{1}{4}x^2$	$y = -2x^2$	$y = 4x^2$
–6	9	–72	144
–4	4	–32	64
–2	1	–8	16
0	0	0	0
2	1	–8	16
4	4	–32	64
6	9	–72	144

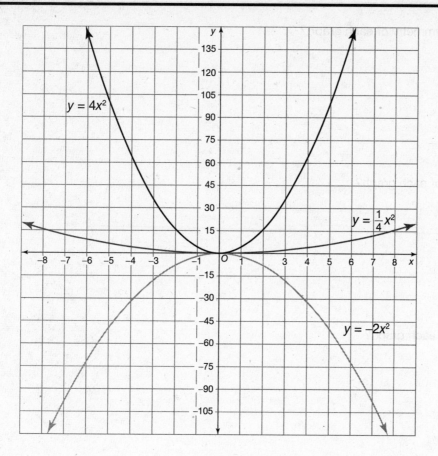

2. Use the graphs and equations above to explain how you know whether a quadratic function opens up or down.

3. Find the vertex of each function.

$y = \dfrac{1}{4}x^2$:

$y = -2x^2$:

$y = 4x^2$:

4. How do you know whether a quadratic function has a minimum or maximum value? Find the minimum or maximum value of each function.

$y = \dfrac{1}{4}x^2$:

$y = -2x^2$:

$y = 4x^2$:

© 2006 Carnegie Learning, Inc.

5. What is the axis of symmetry of each graph?

$y = \dfrac{1}{4}x^2$:

$y = -2x^2$:

$y = 4x^2$:

6. What is the domain of each graph?

$y = \dfrac{1}{4}x^2$:

$y = -2x^2$:

$y = 4x^2$:

7. What is the range of each graph?

$y = \dfrac{1}{4}x^2$:

$y = -2x^2$:

$y = 4x^2$:

8. Compare each graph above. What effect does the coefficient of have on the graph of the function?

9.1 The Museum of Natural History
Powers and Prime Factorization

Students should be able to answer these questions after Lesson 9.1:

- Can you list the factors of a number?
- Can you write the prime factorization of a number?

Directions

Read Question 1 and its solution. Then, in Questions 2 through 4, list all the factors of the given number and tell whether it is a prime or composite number.

1. What are the factors of 24? Is 24 a prime number or a composite number?

   Step 1　　Write 24 as a product of two whole numbers in all possible ways.

   $1 \cdot 24 \quad 2 \cdot 12 \quad 3 \cdot 8 \quad 4 \cdot 6$

   Step 2　　List the factors.

   The factors of 24 are 1, 2, 3, 4, 6, 8, 12, and 24. Because 24 has more than two whole number factors, it is a composite number.

2. 45　　　　　　　　　　3. 81　　　　　　　　　　4. 61

Read Question 5 and its solution. Then, write the prime factorization of each number in Questions 6 through 8. Write your answers as products of powers.

5. Write the prime factorization of 180. Write your answer as a product of powers.

   Step 1　　Write 180 as a product of prime factors.

   $180 = 2 \cdot 2 \cdot 3 \cdot 3 \cdot 5$

   Step 2　　Write the prime factorization as a product of powers.

   $180 = 2^2 \cdot 3^2 \cdot 5$

6. 100　　　　　　　　　　7. 245　　　　　　　　　　8. 86

Read Question 9 and its solution. Then, use prime factorization to find the common factors of each pair of number in Questions 10 through 12.

9. Find the common factors of 28 and 42.

   Step 1　　Write the prime factorization of each number.

   $28 = 2^2 \cdot 7 \qquad 42 = 2 \cdot 3 \cdot 7$

   Step 2　　Each number has 2 and 7 as common factors. The common factors are 2, 7, and $2 \cdot 7 = 14$.

10. 27 and 45　　　　　　　11. 51 and 18　　　　　　　12. 23 and 56

9.2 Bits and Bytes
Multiplying and Dividing Powers

Students should be able to answer these questions after Lesson 9.2:

■ What is the rule for dividing powers with the same base?

■ What is the rule for multiplying powers with the same base?

Directions

Read Question 1 and its solution. Then, simplify each expression in Questions 2 through 7.

1. Simplify the expression $\dfrac{3^8}{3^3}$.

   Step 1   Use the rule for dividing powers having the same base.

   $$\dfrac{3^8}{3^3} = 3^{8-3} \qquad \text{Subtract exponents.}$$

   $$= 3^5 \qquad\qquad \text{Simplify.}$$

2. $\dfrac{7^{12}}{7^{10}}$

3. $\dfrac{13^{17}}{13^{16}}$

4. $\dfrac{9^4}{4^4}$

5. $\dfrac{18^8}{18^1}$

6. $\dfrac{x^{15}}{x^6}$

7. $\dfrac{16x^7}{2x^2}$

Read Question 8 and its solution. Then, simplify each expression in Questions 9 through 14.

8. Simplify the expression .

   Step 1   Use the rule for multiplying powers having the same base.

   $$5^6 5^4 = 5^{6+4} \qquad \text{Add exponents.}$$

   $$= 5^{10} \qquad\qquad \text{Simplify.}$$

9. $3^1 3^5$

10. $1^{12} 1^8$

11. $9^6 6^9$

12. $x^7 x^7$

13. $2y^3 \cdot 3y$

14. $(3x^3)(4y^5)$

9.3 As Time Goes By
Zero and Negative Exponents

Students should be able to answer this question after Lesson 9.3:

- Can you evaluate powers with positive, negative, and zero exponents?

Directions

Read Question 1 and its solution. Then, use what you have learned so far in this chapter to simplify each expression completely in Questions 2 through 10. Write variable expressions with positive exponents.

1. Simplify the expression completely.

   Step 1 $5^0 \cdot 2^{-4} = 1 \cdot 2^{-4}$ A nonzero number to the zero power is 1.

   Step 2 $= \dfrac{1}{2^4}$ $a^{-n} = \dfrac{1}{a^n}$

   Step 3 $= \dfrac{1}{16}$ Simplify.

2. $\dfrac{3^5}{3^8}$

3. $8^{-10}8^{10}$

4. $\dfrac{6^{-1}}{6^2}$

5. $4^{-5}4^7$

6. $\dfrac{x^{-8}}{x^{-9}}$

7. $(4y^3)(3y^{-3})$

8. $\dfrac{3^3x^5}{3x^9}$

9. $\dfrac{5x^{-8}}{3x^8}$

10. $(2x) \cdot \left(\dfrac{x^6}{4x^7}\right)$

Students should be able to answer these questions after Lesson 9.4:

■ How are very large numbers and very small numbers written using scientific notation?

■ What is the difference between scientific notation and standard notation?

Directions

Read Question 1 and its solution. Then, rewrite each number in Questions 2 through 7 in standard form.

1. Rewrite 3.667×10^6 and 5.02×10^{-4} in standard form.

   Step 1 $3.667 \times 10^6 = 3,667,000$ The exponent is *positive*, so move the decimal point 6 places to the *right*.

   Step 2 $5.02 \times 10^{-4} = 0.000502$ The exponent is *negative*, so move the decimal point 4 places to the *left*.

2. 2.3×10^{-5} 3. 6.08×10^3

4. 7.0052×10^8 5. 9.0481×10^{-7}

6. 1.999×10^{-1} 7. 3.93×10^5

Read Question 8 and its solution. Then, rewrite each number in Questions 9 through 13 in scientific notation.

8. Rewrite 13,010 and 0.02506 in scientific notation.

   Step 1 $13,010 = 1.301 \times 10^4$ Move the decimal point 4 places to the *left*.

   Step 2 $0.02506 = 2.506 \times 10^{-2}$ Move the decimal point 2 places to the *right*.

9. 254,000   10. 0.00067

11. 0.001058   12. 6800

13. Write the following numbers in order from least to greatest. First, rewrite each number so that it is in scientific notation.

    4.71×10^{-4}, 0.0041, 39.95×10^{-4}, 0.096, 0.442×10^{-3}, 0.084

The Beat Goes On

Properties of Powers

Students should be able to answer this question after Lesson 9.5:

- Can you use the properties of powers to simplify expressions?

Directions

Read Question 1 and its solution. Then, simplify each expression in Questions 2 through 5. Show all your work and identify the property that is used in each step of the solution. The simplified expression should have no negative exponents.

1. Use the properties of powers to simplify each expression.

   a. $(5^7)^2 = 5^{7 \cdot 2}$ Use the power of a power property: $(a^n)^m = a^{n \cdot m}$

   $\quad\quad = 5^{14}$ Simplify.

   b. $(-2x)^3 = (-2)^3 \cdot x^3$ Use the power of a product property: $(a \cdot b)^m = a^m \cdot b^m$

   $\quad\quad = -8x^3$ Simplify.

   c. $\left(\dfrac{3}{4}\right)^2 = \dfrac{3^2}{4^2}$ Use the power of a quotient property: $\left(\dfrac{a}{b}\right)^m = \dfrac{a^m}{b^m}$

   $\quad\quad = \dfrac{9}{16}$ Simplify.

2. $\left(\dfrac{z^6}{z^9}\right)^{-2}$

3. $\dfrac{(x^4)^3}{(x^4)^7}$

4. $\left(\dfrac{2x^2}{3yz^4}\right)^3$

5. $\dfrac{6x^3y^2}{3x^2y} \cdot (5xy^3)^{-1}$

Students should be able to answer these questions after Lesson 9.6:

- Can you find the *n*th root of a number?
- Can you write an expression in radical form?
- Can you write an expression in rational exponent form?

Directions

Read Question 1 and its solution. Then, complete Questions 2 and 3.

1. What is the cube root of 512?

    Step 1   A number *b* is a cube root of a number *a* if $b^3 = a$. What number cubed equals 512?

    8 is the cube root of 512 because $8^3 = 512$.

2. $\sqrt[3]{-1000}$ = _____ because _____$^3 = -1000$

3. $\sqrt[4]{625}$ = _____ because _____$^4 = 625$

Read Question 4 and its solution. Then, write the expressions in Questions 5 through 7 in radical form. Simplify your answer, if possible.

4. Write $25^{5/3}$ in radical form.

Step 1	$25^{5/3} = 25^{(1/3)5}$	Write power as a product.
Step 2	$= (25^{1/3})^5$	Power of a power property
Step 3	$= (\sqrt[3]{25})^5$	$\sqrt[n]{a} = a^{1/n}$

5. $16^{3/2}$ 6. $20^{2/5}$ 7. $x^{3/4}$

Read Question 8 and its solution. Then, write the expressions in Questions 9 through 11 in rational exponent form. Simplify your answer, if possible.

8. Write $(\sqrt[3]{36})^2$ in rational exponent form.

Step 1	$(\sqrt[3]{36})^2 = (36^{1/3})^2$	$\sqrt[n]{a} = a^{1/n}$
Step 2	$= 36^{(1/3)2}$	Power of a power property
Step 3	$= 36^{2/3}$	Simplify power.

9. $(\sqrt[5]{12})^3$ 10. $(\sqrt{45})^2$ 11. $(\sqrt[4]{x})^{12}$

10.1 Water Balloons

Polynomials and Polynomial Functions

Students should be able to answer these questions after Lesson 10.1:

- Can you classify a polynomial by degree and number of terms?
- What is the Vertical Line Test?

Directions

Read Question 1 and its solution. Then, identify the terms and coefficients in Questions 2 through 4.

1. Identify the terms and coefficients of $-8x^2 + 2x^3 - 1$.

   Step 1 Write the polynomial in standard form.

   $$-8x^2 + 2x^3 - 1 = 2x^3 + (-8)x^2 + (-1)$$

   Step 2 The terms are $2x^3$, $-8x^2$, and -1.

   Step 3 The coefficients are 2, -8, and -1.

2. $5x^2 - x + 7$ 3. $2x^2 - 3x^3 + 6x$ 4. $4x^2 - 5x^3 - x^4 + 5$

Read Question 5 and its solution. Then, complete the table in Question 6.

5. Classify the polynomial $6x^2 - 3x^3 + 10$ by degree and number of terms.

   Step 1 Write the polynomial in standard form.

   $$6x^2 - 3x^3 + 10 = -3x^3 + 6x^2 + 10$$

   Step 2 The highest exponent is 3, so the degree is 3. A polynomial of degree 3 is called a cubic polynomial.

   Step 3 The polynomial has 3 terms, so it is a trinomial.

6.

Polynomial	Degree	Classified by degree	Classified by number of terms
$16x$			
$3x^2 - 16$			
-9			
$-4x^3 + 7x^2 - 2x + 8$			
$-2x + 8$			

7. How do you use the Vertical Line Test to determine whether an equation is a function?

10.2 Play Ball!
Adding and Subtracting Polynomials

Students should be able to answer these questions after Lesson 10.2:

- How do you add polynomials?
- How do you subtract polynomials?

Directions

Read Question 1 and its solution. Then, find each sum in Questions 2 through 5. Write your answers in standard form.

1. Find the sum of $(5x^3 + 2x^2 - 8x + 5)$ and $(3x^3 - x^2 - 8)$.

   Step 1   Group like terms.

   $(5x^3 + 2x^2 - 8x + 5) + (3x^3 - x^2 - 8) = (5x^3 + 3x^3) + (2x^2 - x^2) + (-8x) + (5 - 8)$

   Step 2   Simplify each group of like terms.

   $= 8x^3 + x^2 + (-8x) - 3$

2. $(x^2 - 16) + (3x - 6x^2)$

3. $(8x^2 + 5x - 4) + (25 - 10x^2)$

4. $(5x^2 + x^3 + 4x) + (-2x^2 - x^3)$

5. $(2x^2 + 7x - 3) + (-6x^2 - 3x + 8)$

Read Question 6 and its solution. Then, find each difference in Questions 7 through 10. Write your answers in standard form.

6. Find the difference of $(5x^3 + 2x^2 - 8x + 5)$ and $(3x^3 - x^2 - 8)$.

   Step 1   Distribute the negative sign to each term in the second function.

   $(5x^3 + 2x^2 - 8x + 5) - (3x^3 - x^2 - 8) = 5x^3 + 2x^2 - 8x + 5 - 3x^3 + x^2 + 8$

   Step 2   Group like terms.

   $= (5x^3 - 3x^3) + (2x^2 + x^2) + (-8x) + (5 + 8)$

   Step 3   Simplify each group of like terms.

   $= 2x^3 + 3x^2 - 8x + 13$

7. $(7x^2 + 9) - (2x + 8x^2)$

8. $(3x^2 - 13 + 9x) - (-4x^2 + 9x)$

9. $(11x^2 + 8x - 9) - (-3x^2 - x - 7)$

10. $(-5x^3 - 4x + 10) - (2x^2 + x^3 + 3x)$

10.3 Se Habla Español

Multiplying and Dividing Polynomials

Students should be able to answer these questions after Lesson 10.3:

- Can you use the distributive property to multiply polynomials?
- Can you use long division to divide polynomials?

Directions

Read Question 1 and its solution. Then, find each product in Questions 2 through 5.

1. Find the product $(x - 4)(2x + 1)$.

   Step 1 $(x - 4)(2x + 1) = x(2x + 1) - 4(2x + 1)$ Apply the distributive property.

   Step 2 $= 2x^2 + x - 8x - 4$ Apply the distributive property a second time.

   Step 3 $= 2x^2 - 7x - 4$ Combine like terms.

2. $(x - 9)(x + 9)$

3. $3x^2(-x - 8)$

4. $(3x + 2)(2x + 7)$

5. $(x + 3)(5x^2 - 7x + 4)$

Read Question 6 and its solution. Then, find each quotient in Questions 7 through 10.

6. Divide $x^2 + 4x + 6$ by $x - 3$.

   Step 1   Find the quotient of the first terms, $x^2 \div x = x$. This is the first term in the quotient. Multiply x and $x - 3$ and subtract the result. (See **Step 1** below.)

   Step 2   Bring down the 6 in the dividend. Find the quotient of $7x$ and x, or 7. This is the next term in the quotient. Multiply 7 and $x - 3$ and subtract the result. (See **Step 2** below.)

   Step 3   Write the remainder, 27, over the divisor, $x - 3$, in the quotient. (See **Step 3** below.)

$$
\begin{array}{r}
x + 7 + \frac{27}{x-3} \\
x - 3 \overline{\smash{)}\, x^2 + 4x + 6} \\
\underline{-(x^2 - 3x)} \qquad \text{Step 1} \\
7x + 6 \\
\underline{-(7x - 21)} \qquad \text{Step 2} \\
27
\end{array}
$$

10

7. $(x^2 - 2x - 24) \div (x + 4)$

8. $(3x^2 - x + 2) \div (x - 6)$

9. $(6x^2 + 11x + 4) \div (2x + 1)$

10. $(2x^3 - 4x^2 + 2) \div (x^2 - 16)$

10.4 Making Stained Glass

Multiplying Binomials

Students should be able to answer these questions after Lesson 10.4:

- Can you use the FOIL pattern to multiply binomials?
- What are the special product patterns?

Directions

Read Question 1 and its solution. Then, use the FOIL pattern to find each product in Questions 2 through 5.

1. Use the FOIL pattern to find the product $(x - 5)(2x + 7)$.

   Step 1   Multiply the First terms: $x(2x) = 2x^2$

   Step 2   Multiply the Outer terms: $x(7) = 7x$

   Step 3   Multiply the Inner terms: $(-5)(2x) = -10x$

   Step 4   Multiply the Last terms: $(-5)(7) = -35$

   Step 5   Simplify: $(x - 5)(2x + 7) = 2x^2 + 7x - 10x - 35 = 2x^2 - 3x - 35$

2. $(x + 8)(x + 6)$

3. $(3x - 1)(x - 9)$

4. $(2x + 7)(2x - 9)$

5. $(3x - 2)(4x + 5)$

Read Question 6 and its solution. Then, use the special product patterns to find each product in Questions 7 through 10.

6. Use the sum and difference pattern to find the product $(2x + 3)(2x - 3)$.

   Step 1   The formula for the sum and difference pattern is $(a + b)(a - b) = a^2 - b^2$.

   Step 2   Substitute $2x$ for a and 3 for b and simplify.

              $(2x + 3)(2x - 3) = (2x)^2 - 3^2 = 4x^2 - 9$

> ### Special Product Patterns
>
> Sum and difference pattern:
>
> $(a + b)(a - b) = a^2 - b^2$
>
> Square of a binomial pattern:
>
> $(a + b)^2 = a^2 + 2ab + b^2$
> $(a - b)^2 = a^2 - 2ab + b^2$

7. $(3x - 5)^2$

8. $(6x + 4)(6x - 4)$

9. $(3x - 8y)(3x + 8y)$

10. $(2x + 7y)^2$

10.5 Suspension Bridges

Factoring Polynomials

Students should be able to answer these questions after Lesson 10.5:

■ Can you factor a polynomial by factoring out a common factor?

■ Can you factor polynomials of the form $x^2 + bx + c$?

■ Can you factor polynomials of the form $ax^2 + bx + c$?

Directions

Read Question 1 and its solution. Then, factor each polynomial in Questions 2 through 5 completely.

1. Factor $2x^3 - 6x$ c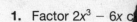

   Step 1 $2x^3$ ... $(x^2) - 2x(3)$ Factor out the common factor $2x$ from each term.

   Step 2   ... $- 3)$ Rewrite using the distributive property.

2. $-3x^2 + 9$ 3. $6x^4 - 15x^2$

4. $8x^3 + 12x^2 - 6x$ 5. $16x^3 + 24x^2$

Read Question 6 and its solution. Then, factor each polynomial in Questions 7 through 10 as a product of linear factors. Use the FOIL pattern to verify your answers.

6. Factor $x^2 - 7x + 12$ as a product of linear factors.

   Step 1 $x^2 - 7x + 12 = (x + a)(x + b)$ Find a and b such that $a + b = -7$ and $ab = 12$.

   Step 2 $= (x - 4)(x - 3)$ $a = -4$ and $b = -3$

   Step 3   Check your answer using the FOIL pattern.

   $(x - 4)(x - 3) = x^2 - 3x - 4x + 12$

   $= x^2 - 7x + 12$

7. $x^2 + 7x + 10$ 8. $x^2 - 3x - 18$

9. $x^2 + 5x - 14$ 10. $x^2 - 64$

Read Question 11 and its solution. Then, factor each polynomial in Questions 12 and 13 as a product of linear factors. Use the FOIL pattern to verify your answers.

11. Factor $3x^2 + 16x + 5$ as a product of linear factors.

   Step 1   Test the possible factors of 3 (3 and 1) and 5 (5 and 1).

   Step 2   Try $(x + 1)(3x + 5)$.

   $(x + 1)(3x + 5) = 3x^2 + 5x + 3x + 5$ This is not the correct factorization.

   $= 3x^2 + 8x + 5$

   Step 3   Try $(x + 5)(3x + 1)$.

   $(x + 5)(3x + 1) = 3x^2 + 15x + x + 5$ This is the correct factorization.

   $= 3x^2 + 16x + 5$

12. $2x^2 + x - 15$

13. $3x^2 - 20x - 7$

10

Swimming Pools

Rational Expressions

Students should be able to answer these questions after Lesson 10.6:

- Can you simplify rational expressions?
- Can you add, subtract, multiply, and divide rational expressions?

Directions

Read Question 1 and its solution. Then, simplify each rational expression in Questions 2 and 3. Restrict the domain so that the simplified expression is equivalent to the original expression.

1. Simplify the expression $\dfrac{x^3 + 2x^2}{x^2 + x - 2}$. Then restrict the domain so that the simplified expression is equivalent to the original expression.

   Step 1 $\quad \dfrac{x^3 + 2x^2}{x^2 + x - 2} = \dfrac{x^2(x + 2)}{(x + 2)(x - 1)} \qquad$ Factor the numerator and the denominator.

   Step 2 $\quad = \dfrac{x^2\cancel{(x + 2)}}{\cancel{(x + 2)}(x - 1)} \qquad$ Divide out the common factor $x + 2$.

   Step 3 $\quad = \dfrac{x^2}{x - 1}, x \neq -2 \qquad$ Restrict the domain. $x \neq -2$ because -2 makes the denominator 0 in the original expression.

2. $\dfrac{x^2 - x - 20}{x^2 - 5x}$

3. $\dfrac{2x^2 + 6x}{x^2 - 9}$

Read Question 4 and its solution. Then, find each product in Questions 5 and 6. Simplify and restrict the domain, if necessary.

4. Find the product $\dfrac{x - 5}{7} \cdot \dfrac{x}{x^2 - 25}$.

   Step 1 $\quad \dfrac{x - 5}{7} \cdot \dfrac{x}{x^2 - 25} = \dfrac{x(x - 5)}{7(x^2 - 25)} \qquad$ Multiply the numerators and denominators.

   Step 2 $\quad = \dfrac{x(x - 5)}{7(x - 5)(x + 5)} \qquad$ Factor.

   Step 3 $\quad = \dfrac{x}{7(x + 5)}, x \neq 5 \qquad$ Divide out the common factor, $x - 5$, and restrict the domain.

5. $\dfrac{2x + 8}{6x} \cdot \dfrac{x^2}{x^2 + 6x + 8}$

6. $\dfrac{x^3 - 4x^2 - 5x}{2x} \cdot \dfrac{x + 1}{4x - 20}$

Read Question 7 and its solution. Then, find each quotient in Questions 8 and 9. Simplify and restrict the domain, if necessary.

7. Find the quotient $\dfrac{x^2 - 2x - 8}{x^2 + 12x + 36} \div \dfrac{3x - 12}{x + 6}$.

Step 1 $\quad \dfrac{x^2 - 2x - 8}{x^2 + 12x + 36} \div \dfrac{3x - 12}{x + 6}$

$\quad = \dfrac{x^2 - 2x - 8}{x^2 + 12x + 36} \cdot \dfrac{x + 6}{3x - 12}$ Multiply by the reciprocal.

Step 2 $\quad = \dfrac{(x^2 - 2x - 8)(x + 6)}{(x^2 + 12x + 36)(3x + 12)}$ Multiply.

Step 3 $\quad = \dfrac{(x - 4)(x + 2)(x + 6)}{3(x + 6)(x + 6)(x - 4)}$ Factor.

Step 4 $\quad = \dfrac{x + 2}{3(x + 6)}, x \neq 4$ Divide out the common factors and restrict the domain.

8. $\dfrac{6}{x - 3} \div \dfrac{x^2 + 3x - 18}{x^2 - 6x + 9}$

9. $\dfrac{x^2 - 8x + 7}{12x} \div \dfrac{x^2 - 6x - 7}{4x + 12}$

Read Question 10 and its solution. Then, find the sum or difference in Questions 11 and 12. Simplify your answer.

10. Find the difference $\dfrac{9}{x} - \dfrac{4}{5x}$.

Step 1 $\quad \dfrac{9}{x} - \dfrac{4}{5x} = \dfrac{9}{x} \cdot \dfrac{5}{5} - \dfrac{4}{5x}$ Multiply by an appropriate form of 1.

Step 2 $\quad = \dfrac{45}{5x} - \dfrac{4}{5x}$ Multiply.

Step 3 $\quad = \dfrac{45 - 4}{5x}$ Subtract.

Step 4 $\quad = \dfrac{41}{5x}$ Simplify.

11. $\dfrac{7}{6x} + \dfrac{5}{9}$

12. $\dfrac{2x}{x + 4} - \dfrac{3}{4}$

Students should be able to answer these questions after Lesson 11.1:

■ How do you find the probability of an event?

■ How do you find the odds that an event will happen?

■ What is the difference between probability and odds?

Directions

Read Question 1 and its solution. Then, use your understanding of probability and odds to complete Questions 2 through 4.

1. An internet site devoted to local weather predicted that two of the days next week will be rainy. What is the probability that it will be rainy on a given day next week? What are the odds that it will be rainy on any given day next week?

    To find the probability of an event, find the ratio of the number of favorable outcomes to

    the number of possible outcomes. Probability $= \dfrac{\text{Number of favorable outcomes}}{\text{Number of possible outcomes}}$

    Step 1 There are 7 days in a week. So, the total number of outcomes is 7.

    Step 2 Two of the days are expected to be rainy. So, the number of favorable outcomes is 2.

    The probability that it will be rainy on a given day next week is $\dfrac{2}{7}$.

    To find the odds that an event will occur, find the ratio of the number of favorable

    outcomes to the number of unfavorable outcomes. Odds in favor $= \dfrac{\text{Number of favorable coutcomes}}{\text{Number of unfavorable outcomes}}$

    Step 1 Two of the days are expected to be rainy. So, the number of favorable outcomes is 2.

    Step 2 Five of the days are expected to not be rainy. So, the number of unfavorable outcomes is 5.

    The odds that it will be rainy on a given day next week are $\dfrac{2}{5}$.

2. If you roll a six-sided number cube, what is the probability that it will land on 5? What are the odds that the number cube will land on 5?

3. As part of their ten-year promotional campaign, a local store proudly announces that 1 in 5 shoppers will win a prize. What are the odds that a given shopper will win a prize?

11

4. A television show is choosing winners in its talent search. They have narrowed their search down to 4 girls and 3 boys. What is the probability that they will choose a girl? What are the odds that they will choose a girl?

11.2 What's In the Bag?
Experimental and Theoretical Probabilities

Students should be able to answer these questions after Lesson 11.2:
- How do you find an experimental probability?
- What is the relationship between experimental and theoretical probability?

Directions

Read Question 1 and its solution. Then, use your understanding of probability and odds to complete the Question 2 through 4.

1. A bag contains colored tiles. There are 5 red tiles, 5 blue tiles, and 5 orange tiles. Suppose that you randomly choose a tile from the bag. How many times would you expect to select a red tile?

   Step 1 Because you are making a prediction about the event and you know all of the possible outcomes that are equally likely to occur, you are finding a theoretical probability.

   Step 2 The theoretical probability is the ratio of the number of favorable outcomes to the number of possible outcomes. So, the theoretical probability of selecting a red tile from the bag is

   $$\text{Theoretical Probability} = \frac{\text{Number of favorable outcomes}}{\text{Number of possible outcomes}} = \frac{5 \text{ red tiles}}{15 \text{ tiles}} = \frac{1}{3}$$

2. Suppose that you randomly choose a tile from the bag and then replace the tile 10 times. You select 2 red tiles, 4 blue tiles, and 4 orange tiles. Calculate the experimental probability of selecting a blue tile.

   $$\text{Experimental Probability} = \frac{\text{Number of successes}}{\text{Number of trials}}$$

3. Perform an experiment by flipping a coin 20 times. Then find the theoretical and experimental probability of a coin landing on tails after being flipped 20 times.

4. Suppose that you roll a six-sided number cube 6 times. Find the theoretical and experimental probability that the number cube lands on 2.

A Brand New Bag

Using Probabilities to Make Predictions

Students should be able to answer this question after Lesson 11.3:

■ How are experiments used to make predictions?

Directions

Read Question 1 and its solution. Then complete Question 2.

1. Suppose that you and your friend run an experiment. Your friend tears a piece of paper into 15 small pieces. The number 1, 2, or 3 is written on each piece of paper. The pieces of paper are placed into a bag. You randomly select a piece of paper from the bag, record the number, and return it to the bag. The table below shows the results of choosing a piece of paper 20 times. Find the experimental probability of choosing a piece of paper with each number written on it. Then find the number of pieces of paper with each number written on them.

Piece of paper	1	2	3
Number of times paper was chosen	4	13	3

Step 1   Find the experimental probability for choosing a piece of paper with each number on it.

Probability of choosing a 1 $= \dfrac{4}{20} = \dfrac{1}{5}$ Probability of choosing a 2 $= \dfrac{13}{20}$

Probability of choosing a 3 $= \dfrac{3}{20}$

Step 2   Use the results from step one to determine the number of each kind of piece of paper that is in the bag.

"1" pieces of paper: $15\left(\dfrac{1}{5}\right) = 3$ "2" pieces of paper: $15\left(\dfrac{13}{20}\right) = 9\dfrac{3}{4}$

"3" pieces of paper: $15\left(\dfrac{3}{20}\right) = 2\dfrac{1}{4}$

So, there are about 3 pieces of paper with "1" written on them, about 10 pieces of paper with "2" written on them, and about 2 pieces of paper with "3" written on them.

2. Suppose that your friend had started with 40 pieces of paper and that you randomly choose a piece of paper from the bag 20 times and replaced it. You found 12 pieces of paper with "1" written on them, 6 pieces of paper with "2" written on them, and 2 pieces of paper with "3" written on them. Use the experimental probabilities to predict the total number of each kind of piece of paper that is in the bag.

Fun With Number Cubes

Graphing Frequencies of Outcomes

Students should be able to answer these questions after Lesson 11.4:

- How can a line plot be used to help determine probability?
- How are probabilities found and compared?

Directions

Read Question 1 and its solution. Then complete Questions 2 through 4.

1. A game spinner is divided into six regions, each a different size. During the course of a board game, players took turns spinning the spinner and moving around the board. The results of the spins are shown in the line plot below. Find the experimental probability that the spinner will land on Region 2.

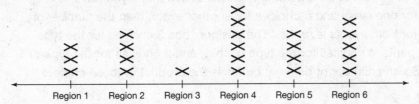

Step 1   Find the number of times the spinner landed on Region 2. Then find the number of times that the spinner was spun.

Count the number of X's above Region 2. There are 4 X's, so the spinner landed on Region 2 four times. Count the number of X's in the line plot. There are 23 X's in the line plot, so the spinner was spun 23 times.

Step 2   Find the experimental probability that the spinner will land on Region 2.

The experimental probability that the spinner will land on Region 2 is the ratio of the number of times the spinner landed on Region 2 to the total number of times the spinner was spun, or $\frac{4}{23}$.

2. Find the experimental probability that the spinner will land on Region 1.

3. Based on the results, which region of the spinner would you guess is the largest? Explain your reasoning.

4. Based on the results, which region of the spinner would you guess is the smallest? Explain your reasoning.

11

11.5 Going To The Movies
Counting and Permutations

Students should be able to answer these questions after Lesson 11.5:
- What is a permutation?
- How is the Fundamental Counting Principle used to solve problem situations?

Directions

Read Question 1 and its solution. Then complete Questions 2 through 4.

1. A designer offers a line of clothing with 3 types of dress pants, 4 shirts, and 2 blazers. How many different outfits can be made from this line of clothing?

   Step 1　Use the Fundamental Counting Principle to find the number of different outfits. The Fundamental Counting Principle states that if you have m choices for one event and n choices for another event, then the number of choices for both events is $m \cdot n$. The designer has 3 choices for the type of dress pants, 4 choices for the type of shirt, and 2 choices for the type of blazer. So, the number of different outfits is the product of these choices.

   $3 \cdot 4 \cdot 2 = 24$

   There are 24 different outfits that can be made from this line of clothing.

2. An interior designer is trying to find the best combination of paint color, window treatments, and flooring for a room. He has narrowed his list down to 4 different wall colors, 5 different window treatments, and 2 types of flooring. How many different ways can the interior designer design the room?

3. A photographer can choose from 3 different types of prints and 4 different picture frames. How many different options are available for the next picture that she will frame?

4. You are making cheese sandwiches for a luncheon. Each sandwich will use 1 type of bread and 1 type of cheese. You can choose whole wheat, honey, multi-grain, or cinnamon bread. You can choose Swiss cheese, American cheese, provolone cheese, or cheddar cheese. How many different sandwiches can be made?

Going Out For Pizza

Permutations and Combinations

Students should be able to answer these questions after Lesson 11.6:

■ How are permutations determined in a problem situation?

■ How is the formula for permutations different from the formula for combinations?

■ What is the difference between a combination and a permutation?

Directions

Read Question 1 and its solution. Then, complete Questions 2 through 7.

1. An interior designer has narrowed the colors that he may use to decorate the first floor of a house to 5 different colors. The first floor has 3 different rooms, and he would like them all to be painted different colors. How many different color combinations are available to the designer if order is not important? In how many ways can the designer paint the rooms?

Step 1 The first question asks about the number of color combinations. So, use the combinations formula. In this problem, you are finding the number of combinations of 5 colors of paint taken 3 at a time.

$$_nC_r = \frac{n!}{(n-r)!}$$

$$_5C_3 = \frac{5!}{(5-3)!3!} = \frac{5!}{2!3!} = \frac{5 \cdot 4 \cdot 3 \cdot 2 \cdot 1}{(2 \cdot 1)(3 \cdot 2 \cdot 1)} = 5 \cdot 2 = 10$$

Step 2 The second question asks about the ways to paint the rooms. In this question, order is important, so use the permutations formula. In this problem, you are finding the number of permutations of 5 colors of paint taken 3 at a time.

$$_nP_r = \frac{n!}{(n-r)!}$$

$$_5P_3 = \frac{5!}{(5-3)!} = \frac{5!}{2!} = \frac{5 \cdot 4 \cdot 3 \cdot 2 \cdot 1}{2 \cdot 1} = 60$$

2. Find the value of $_4P_3$.

3. Find the value of $_{10}P_2$.

4. Find the value of $_6C_2$.

5. Find the value of $_7C_4$.

6. Find the value of $_5P_5$.

7. Find the value of $_3C_3$.

11

11.7

11.7 Picking Out Socks

Independent and Dependent Events

Students should be able to answer these questions after Lesson 11.7:

■ How is the probability of compound events determined?

■ What is the difference between independent and dependent events?

Directions

Read Question 1 and its solution. Then complete Questions 2 through 4.

1. One hundred raffle tickets were sold as a fundraiser. Tickets will be randomly selected from a hat to determine who wins each of 3 prizes. Once a raffle ticket has been selected, it is not put back in the hat. The grand prize is a giant gift basket filled with different types of candy. You bought 3 tickets, your sister bought 10 tickets, your brother bought 5 tickets, your uncle bought 2 tickets, and your teacher bought 1 ticket. What is the probability that you and your brother will both win prizes?

Step 1 Determine whether the events are dependent or independent.

Because each raffle ticket is permanently removed from the hat after being selected, the second event depends upon the first.

Step 2 Find the probability that you and your brother will both win prizes.

The probability that one of your raffle tickets will be selected is $\frac{3}{100}$ and the probability that one of your brother's raffle tickets will be selected is $\frac{5}{99}$.

Find the product of the probabilities.

The probability that you and your brother will both win prizes is

$$\frac{3}{100} \cdot \frac{5}{99} = \frac{1}{660}.$$

2. What is the probability that you and your teacher will both win a prize?

3. What is the probability that your uncle will win two prizes?

4. Suppose that the tickets where randomly selected from the hat and then returned to the hat. Are the events dependent or independent? What is the probability that your brother and sister would both win prizes?

11

Probability on the Shuffleboard Court

Geometric Probabilities

Students should be able to answer these questions after Lesson 11.8:

■ How is the geometric probability of an event determined?

■ How is geometric probability used in a problem situation?

Directions

Read Question 1 and its solution. Then complete Questions 2 through 4.

1. A person is blindfolded and led to a game board. She will win a prize if she places the game piece on the bull's-eye. The bull's-eye is 40 square centimeters while the rest of the board takes up about 360 square centimeters. What is the probability that she will randomly place the piece onto the bull's-eye?

   Step 1 The geometric probability is the ratio of the area of the bull's-eye to the total area. The bull's-eye is 40 square centimeters and the total area is 40 + 360 square centimeters. So, the probability that the person will randomly place the game piece on the bull's-eye is $\frac{40}{400} = \frac{1}{10}$.

2. Suppose that a game board is divided into six triangles, where each triangle has the same area. What is the probability that a number cube will land on one particular triangle?

3. Suppose that a game board is divided into four sections of equal size, but different colors. The colors are red, blue, green, and yellow. If you roll a number cube 24 times, how often would you expect it to land on the yellow section?

4. How would you relate the formula for geometric probability to the formula for probability that has been used in previous lessons?

11

11.9 Game Design
Geometric Probabilities and Fair Games

Students should be able to answer this question after Lesson 11.9:
■ How is geometric probability used to determine values in a game?

Read Question 1 and its solution. Then complete Questions 2 through 4.

1. A friend designed a game for the two of you to play. It consists of two concentric circles at which you will randomly throw darts. The inner region is the bull's-eye that takes up $\frac{1}{3}$ of the total area and is worth 100 points. The outer region is worth 50 points and takes up $\frac{2}{3}$ of the area. Suppose that you throw a dart 50 times. How many times would you expect to hit the bull's-eye?

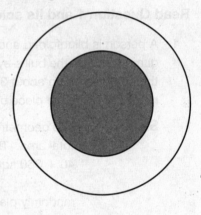

   Step 1   Because the bull's-eye takes up of the total area, the probability that you will throw one dart and hit the bull's-eye is $\frac{1}{3}$.

   Step 2   If you throw a dart 50 times, then the number of times that you can expect to hit the bull's-eye is about 16 because $50\left(\frac{1}{3}\right) = 16\frac{2}{3}$.

2. Suppose that your friend throws a dart 75 times. How many times can your friend expect to hit the outer region?

3. What is the probability that you will score 300 points on three tries?

4. What is the probability that you will earn a score of 150 on two tries?

12.1 Taking the PSAT

Measures of Central Tendency

Students should be able to answer these questions after Lesson 12.1:

- Can you find the mean, median, and mode of a data set?
- What information can readily be seen from a stem-and-leaf plot?

Directions

Read Question 1 and its solution. Then, use the scenario to complete Questions 2 through 7.

1. Students taking the physical fitness test in gym class are required to do curl-ups, or sit-ups. The number of curl-ups completed in one minute for a girls' gym class are shown below. Make a stem-and-leaf plot of the data.

   25, 37, 19, 20, 28, 37, 40, 27, 46, 44, 52, 17, 39, 22, 29, 33, 27, 38, 31, 41, 27

   Step 1   Let the stem represent the 10s digit. Let the leaf represent the ones digit.

   Step 2   Make the stem-and-leaf plot, displaying the data in numerical order. Include a key.

1	79
2	02577789
3	137789
4	0146
5	2

   $2 \mid 5 = 25$

2. What is the most number of curl-ups? What is the least number of curl-ups?

3. What type of distribution does the data have (symmetric, skewed left, skewed right)?

4. What is the mean, or average, number of curl-ups?

5. Use the stem-and-leaf plot in Question 1 to find the median, or middle, number of curl-ups.

6. What is the mode of the data?

7. Which measure of central tendency, the median or the mode, is the better representation of the number of curl-ups? Explain your answer.

12

Students should be able to answer these questions after Lesson 12.2:

■ Can you find the mean and median of a data set?

■ How do data values affect the mean and median of a data set?

Directions

The table below shows sample data from a survey that asked people to rate school subjects. Use the data to complete Questions 1 through 3.

This is one of my favorite subjects.	9–10
I usually like this subject.	7–8
This subject is OK.	5–6
I usually dislike this subject.	3–4
This is one of my least favorite subjects.	1–2

School subject	Reviewer 1 rating	Reviewer 2 rating	Reviewer 3 rating	Reviewer 4 rating	Reviewer 5 rating	Reviewer 6 rating
Mathematics	40	23	5	50	30	25
English	20	32	23	20	20	25
History	30	40	30	25	10	20
Gym	30	10	50	15	45	20
Art	45	40	35	43	10	30

1. Find the mean rating and the median rating for each school subject. Round your answers to the nearest tenth if necessary.

2. Are the mean rating and the median rating close together for any of the subjects? Use a complete sentence in your answer.

3. With which single reviewer do you agree with the least? Replace all of his ratings with your own ratings in that reviewer's column. Find the new mean rating and new median rating for each school subject. Has the relationship between the mean and median changed for any of the subjects? If so, in what way has it changed?

12

12.3 Breakfast Cereals

Quartiles and Box-and-Whisker Plots

Students should be able to answer these questions after Lesson 12.3:

- Can you represent data using a box-and-whisker plot?
- What is an outlier of a data set?

Directions

Read Question 1 and its solution. Then, complete Questions 2 through 4.

1. Draw a box-and-whisker plot of the data set below.

   19, 5, 24, 49, 36, 27, 18, 34, 28, 16

   Step 1   Write the numbers in increasing order.

   5, 16, 18, 19, 24, 27, 28, 34, 36, 49

   Step 2   Find the median, or second quartile (Q_2).

   $$\frac{24 + 27}{2} = 25.5$$

   Step 3   Find the median of the lower half, or the first quartile (Q_1).

   The median of 5, 16, 18, 19, 24 is 18.

   Step 4   Find the median of the upper half, or the third quartile (Q_3).

   The median of 27, 28, 34, 36, 49 is 34.

   Step 5   Use a number line to plot the lower extreme, Q_1, Q_2, Q_3, and the upper extreme.

   Draw a box-and-whisker plot as shown below.

   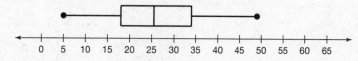

2. You are a waitress at a restaurant. You earned the following weekly tips (in dollars) in 12 weeks. Draw a box-and-whisker plot of the data.

   190, 166, 154, 204, 125, 180, 210, 175, 164, 180, 165, 178

3. What is the outlier in Question 2? Remove the outlier and find Q_1, Q_2, and Q_3.

4. Find the interquartile range ($Q_3 - Q_1$) of the data in Question 2. What does this number represent?

Home Team Advantage?

Sample Variance and Standard Deviation

Students should be able to answer these questions after Lesson 12.4:

- How is the deviation of a data set calculated, and what does it represent?
- How is the variance of a data set calculated, and what does it represent?
- How is the standard deviation of a data set calculated, and what does it represent?

Directions

Read Question 1 and its solution. Then, use the data to complete Questions 2.

1. Your basketball team is having a foul shooting competition. The 16 members of the team have split up into two teams, the red team and the blue team. Each player shoots 50 foul shots and the number of baskets made is recorded. The results are shown in the table below.

	Player 1	Player 2	Player 3	Player 4	Player 5	Player 6	Player 7	Player 8
Red	37	27	45	34	29	39	30	23
Blue	31	27	20	25	42	40	34	29

a. Find the mean ($\bar{x}$) for the red team.

Step 1 Find the sum and divide by the number of players.

$$\frac{27 + 37 + 45 + 34 + 29 + 39 + 30 + 23}{8} = \frac{264}{8} = 33$$

b. Find the deviation for the red team.

Step 1 Calculate $(x - \bar{x})$ for each player.

1: $37 - 33 = 4$ 2: $27 - 33 = -6$ 3: $45 - 33 = 12$ 4: $34 - 33 = 1$

5: $29 - 33 = -4$ 6: $39 - 33 = 6$ 7: $30 - 33 = -3$ 8: $23 - 33 = -10$

c. Find the sum of the squares of the deviations for the red team.

Step 1 Square the deviation for each player.

1: $4^2 = 16$ 2: $(-6)^2 = 36$ 3: $12^2 = 144$ 4: $1^2 = 1$

5: $(-4)^2 = 16$ 6: $6^2 = 36$ 7: $(-3)^2 = 9$ 8: $(-10)^2 = 100$

Step 2 Add all the squares of the deviations.

$16 + 36 + 144 + 1 + 16 + 36 + 9 + 100 = 358$

d. Find the sample standard deviation for the red team.

Step 1 Divide the sum of the squares of the deviations by the sample size minus 1.

$$\frac{358}{8-1} = \frac{358}{7} \approx 51.14$$

Step 2 Take the square root. $\sqrt{51.14} \approx 7.15$

The standard deviation is about 7.15.

2. Complete parts (A) through (D) above for the blue team.

12

13.1 Solid Carpentry

The Pythagorean Theorem and Its Converse

Students should be able to answer these questions after Lesson 13.1:

■ What is the Pythagorean Theorem?

■ How is the Pythagorean Theorem used to find an unknown side length of a right triangle?

■ How is the converse of the Pythagorean Theorem used to determine whether a triangle is a right triangle?

Directions

Read Question 1 and its solution. Then complete Questions 2 and 3.

1. Ricky and Robby met by the flagpole to play catch. Ricky walked 20 feet north from the flagpole. Robby walked 15 feet west from the flagpole. How far must they throw the ball to reach each other?

   Step 1 Draw a diagram to represent the flagpole and the place where Ricky and Robby are standing.

   Step 2 Use the Pythagorean theorem, which states that if a and b are the side lengths of a right triangle, and c is the hypotenuse, then $a^2 + b^2 = c^2$. In this problem, a is 20 feet, b is 15 feet, and you need to find c.

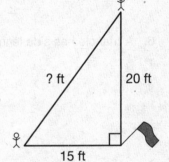

   $$a^2 + b^2 = c^2$$
   $$20^2 + 15^2 = c^2$$
   $$400 + 255 = c^2$$
   $$625 = c^2$$
   $$\sqrt{625} = c$$
   $$25 = c$$

   So, the distance between Ricky and Robby is 25 feet.

2. An 8 foot ladder is propped up against a wall so that the base of the ladder is 5 feet from the wall. How high on the wall does the ladder reach? Round your answer to the nearest tenth of a foot.

3. Candace leaves her home and walks 2 miles south. She then turns and walks 3 miles east. What is the distance from her new location back to her home? Round your answer to the nearest tenth of a mile.

Read Question 4 and its solution. Then complete Questions 5 and 6.

4. A triangle has side lengths 2 centimeters, 5 centimeters, and 7 centimeters. Use the converse of the Pythagorean Theorem to determine whether the triangle is a right triangle.

> **Step 1** The converse of the Pythagorean Theorem states that if three side lengths of a triangle have the relationship $a^2 + b^2 = c^2$, then the triangle is a right triangle. Let a be 2 centimeters, b be 5 centimeters, and c be 7 centimeters.

> **Step 2** Substitute and evaluate each side of the equation.
>
> $2^2 + 5^2 \overset{?}{=} 7^2$
>
> $4 + 25 \overset{?}{=} 49$
>
> $29 \neq 49$
>
> The triangle is not a right triangle, because $2^2 + 5^2 \neq 7^2$.

5. A triangle has side lengths 10 inches, 24 inches, and 26 inches. Is the triangle a right triangle?

6. A triangle has side lengths 1 meter, 2 meters, and 3 meters. Is the triangle a right triangle?

Location, Location, Location
The Distance and Midpoint Formulas

Students should be able to answer these questions after Lesson 13.2:

- What is the Distance formula?
- What is the Midpoint formula?
- How is the Distance formula related to the Pythagorean Theorem?

Directions

Read Question 1 and its solution. Then find the distance and midpoint between each pair of points in Questions 2 through 5.

1. Find the distance between (1, 3) and (5, 6). Then find the midpoint between the points.

   Step 1   Use the distance formula to find the distance between two points.

   The distance formula is $d = \sqrt{(x_2 - x_1)^2 + (y_2 - y_1)^2}$

   $$d = \sqrt{(5 - 1)^2 + (6 - 3)^2}$$
   $$= \sqrt{(4)^2 + (3)^2}$$
   $$= \sqrt{16 + 9}$$
   $$= \sqrt{25} = 5$$

   The distance between the points is 5 units.

   Step 2   Use the midpoint formula to find the point that is halfway between (1, 3) and (5, 6). The midpoint formula is $\left(\dfrac{x_1 + x_2}{2}, \dfrac{y_1 + y_2}{2}\right)$.

   $$\left(\frac{1 + 5}{2}, \frac{3 + 6}{2}\right) = \left(\frac{6}{2}, \frac{9}{2}\right) = \left(3, \frac{9}{2}\right)$$

   So, the midpoint between the points is $\left(3, \dfrac{9}{2}\right)$.

2. (−1, 3) and (4, 5)

3. (0, 0) and (−4, 6)

4. (−5, −9) and (?7, 3)

5. (6, 10) and (−8, 11)

"Old" Mathematics

Completing the Square and Deriving the Quadratic Formula

Students should be able to answer these questions after Lesson 13.3:

■ What is completing the square?

■ When is completing the square an appropriate method to use to solve a quadratic equation?

■ What other methods have you learned for solving a quadratic equation?

Directions

Read Question 1 and its solution. Then solve each equation in Questions 2 through 5 by completing the square and extracting square roots.

1. Solve the equation $x^2 - 2x - 53 = 0$ by completing the square.

Step 1   Note that the equation cannot be factored as it is written. We can make $x^2 - 2x$ a perfect square trinomial, so get this expression on one side of the equation.

$$x^2 - 2x - 53 = 0$$
$$x^2 - 2x = 53$$

Step 2   Add a number to each side of the equation that will make $x^2 - 2x$ a perfect square trinomial. Then factor the left side of the equation.

$$x^2 - 2x + 1 = 53 + 1$$
$$x^2 - 2x + 1 = 54$$
$$(x - 1)^2 = 54$$

Step 3   Extract square roots to solve the equation.

$$x - 1 = \sqrt{54} \qquad\qquad x - 1 = -\sqrt{54}$$
$$x = \sqrt{54} + 1 \qquad\qquad x = -\sqrt{54} + 1$$
$$x \approx 8.348 \qquad\qquad x \approx -6.348$$

2. $x^2 - 12x = -14$

3. $x^2 + 16x + 35 = 0$

4. $x^2 + 18x = -43$

5. $x^2 + 24x = 23$

Learning To Be A Teacher
Vertex Form of a Quadratic Equation

Students should be able to answer these questions after Lesson 13.4:

■ What does it mean for a quadratic equation to be written in vertex form?

■ What information is easily obtained from each of the different forms of a quadratic equation?

Directions

Read Question 1 and its solution. Then complete Questions 2 through 4.

1. Write the quadratic equation $y = x^2 + 6x$ in vertex form. Then identify the vertex.

   Step 1   The vertex form of a quadratic equation is an equation of the form $y = (x - h)^2 + k$ where (h, k) is the vertex of the graph. To rewrite the equation $y = x^2 + 6x$ in vertex form, use the completing the square method.

   $$y = x^2 + 6x$$

   $$y + 9 = x^2 + 6x + 9$$

   $$y + 9 = (x + 3)^2$$

   $$y = (x + 3)^2 - 9$$

   So, the vertex form of the equation is $y = (x + 3)^2 - 9$.

   Step 2   The vertex of the quadratic equation is $(-3, -9)$, because $h = -3$ and $k = -9$.

2. Write the quadratic equation $y = x^2 - 8x + 1$ in vertex form. Then identify the vertex.

3. Write the quadratic equation $y = x^2 - 12x + 40$ in vertex form. Then identify the vertex.

4. The standard form of a quadratic equation is $y = x^2 - 4x + 4$. What is the y-intercept? The factored form of the equation is $y = (x - 2)(x - 2)$. What is the x-intercept? The vertex form of the equation is $y = (x - 2)^2 + 0$. What is the vertex?

Screen Saver

Graphing by Using Parent Functions

Students should be able to answer these questions after Lesson 13.5:

- What are the basic transformations of quadratic functions?
- How do transformations affect the graph of a function?

Directions

Read Question 1 and its solution. Then complete Questions 2 through 5.

1. For the function $y = x^2 + 5$, identify the parent function. Then describe the transformation on the parent function that will result in the graph of the given function.

   Step 1 First, identify the parent function. For the function $y = x^2 + 5$, the parent function is $y = x^2$.

   Step 2 The transformation on the graph of $y = x^2$ that will result in the graph of $y = x^2 + 5$ is a vertical shift up 5 units.

   Note that a function of the form $y = x^2 + n$ results in a vertical shift of n units. A function of the form $y = (x - n)^2$ results in a horizontal shift n units. A function of the form $y = ax^2$ results in a dilation by a factor of a. The sign of a in each form tells you whether the parabola opens upward or downward.

2. For the function $y = (x - 1)^2$, identify the parent function. Then describe the transformation on the parent function that will result in the graph of the given function.

3. For the function $y = (x + 7)^2$, identify the parent function. Then describe the transformation on the parent function that will result in the graph of the given function.

4. For the function $y = 2x^2 + 3$, identify the parent function. Then describe the transformation on the parent function that will result in the graph of the given function.

5. For the function $y = 3(x + 5)^2 - 2$, identify the parent function. Then describe the transformation on the parent function that will result in the graph of the given function.

13.6 Science Fair

Introduction to Exponential Functions

Students should be able to answer these questions after Lesson 13.6:

■ How are exponential functions written?

■ How are exponential functions graphed?

■ How are exponential functions used in real-life problem situations?

Directions

Read Question 1 and its solution. Then complete Questions 2 through 4.

1. Suppose that a scientist begins studying a particular type of bacteria in a petri dish. She begins with 1 bacteria. The population will triple every hour. Write a function that gives the bacterial growth in terms of time. How many bacteria will there be after 2 hours?

   Step 1 The growth of bacteria can be modeled by an exponential function. An exponential function is of the form $y = a^x$, where $a > 0$ and $a \neq 1$. The growth of the bacteria can be modeled by the function $y = 3^x$.

   Step 2 Evaluate the function $y = 3^x$ for $x = 2$ to find the number of bacteria after 2 hours.

   $y = 3^2 = 9$

   So, there will be 9 bacteria after 2 hours.

2. Complete the table below. Note that the log phase is the phase of bacterial growth where the bacteria are growing rapidly. Use the table to graph the data.

Time since beginning of log phase (in hours)	Number of bacteria	Prime fractorization of bacteria
0		
1		
2	9	$(3)^2$
3		
4		
5		

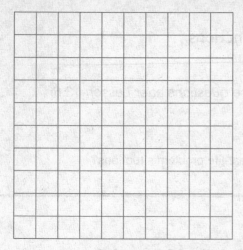

3. What is the *y*-intercept? What does the *y*-intercept represent in the problem situation?

4. On Monday, Sonya received an email. The next day, she sent the email to 5 people. The next day each person sent the email to 5 people. The pattern continues each day. Write a function that gives the total number of emails in terms of the time since Monday. How many emails will have been sent 4 days after Monday?

13.7 Money Comes and Money Goes

Exponential Growth and Decay

Students should be able to answer these questions after Lesson 13.7:

- How are exponential growth and decay functions modeled?
- How are exponential growth and decay functions used in real-life problem situations?

Directions

Read Question 1 and its solution. Then complete Questions 2 through 5.

1. You purchase a digital camera for $300. The camera depreciates at a rate of 30% annually. What is the camera's value after 5 years?

   Step 1 Use the exponential decay model $y = C(1 - r)^t$, where C is the original amount, r is the rate of change, and t is the time. For this problem, C is 300, r is 0.30, and t is 5 years.

   $$y = C(1 - r)^t$$
   $$y = 300(1 - 0.30)^5$$
   $$y \approx 50.421$$

   So, the camera's value after 5 years is about $50.42.

2. You have just bought a set of coins for $150 that will increase in value at a rate of 2% every year. Use the exponential growth model $y = C(1 - r)^t$, where C is the original amount, r is the rate of change, and t is the time to find the value of the coins after 20 years.

3. Your nephew just purchased a rare baseball card that is valued at $250. Suppose that the card's value will increase at a rate of 10% every year. How much will it be worth in 50 years?

4. You purchase a car for $13,500. The car depreciates at a rate of 25% annually. How much will your car be worth after 7 years?

5. Five years ago, you purchased a computer for $2000. Suppose that the computer depreciates at a rate of 30% annually. How much is the computer worth now?

13.8 Camping

Special Topic: Logic

Students should be able to answer these questions after Lesson 13.8:

■ What is a mathematical proof?

■ How is a statement proven indirectly?

■ What is a mathematical contradiction?

Directions

Read Question 1 and its solution. Then tell whether the statements in Questions 2 through 4 are true or false. If the statement is false, use a counterexample in your answer.

1. Prove that the following statement is false by finding a counterexample. If a number is a multiple of 3, then it is always odd.

   Step 1 A counterexample is an example that shows that the statement is not true. For a statement to be true, it has to be true for every single number. One counterexample proves that it is false.

   A counterexample to the statement is the number 30. The number 30 is a multiple of 3, but the number is even. So, the statement is false.

2. In order to purchase a product, you have to go to the store.

3. If a quadrilateral has four right angles, then it is a square.

4. If a number is divisible by 2, then it is also divisible by 4.

Read Question 5 and its solution. Then complete Question 6.

5.

$(a + b)(a - b) = a^2 - b^2$	Original equation
$a^2 + ab - ab - b^2 = a^2 - b^2$	FOIL
$a^2 + 0 - b^2 = a^2 - b^2$	Additive Inverse
$a^2 - b^2 = a^2 - b^2$	Add.

6. Is the statement $(m - n)^2 = m^2 - n^2$ true?

Answers

Chapter 1

Lesson 1.1

2. 2, 4, 6, 8, 10 3. 12

4. 12, 6, 3; Divide the previous term by 2 to get the next term.

5. 81, 243, 729; Multiply the previous term by 3 to get the next term.

6. 20, 15, 10; Subtract 5 from the previous term to get the next term.

Lesson 1.2

2. 2, 2.5, 3, 3.5, …; 7; After 10 hours, there will be 7 inches of snow.

4. 73 5. 27

Lesson 1.3

2. $75; $175; $10n + 25$

4. 100 5. 108

7. $a_1 = 5(1) - 4 = 1$

   $a_2 = 5(2) - 4 = 6$

   $a_3 = 5(3) - 4 = 11$

8. $a_1 = 3(1)^2 + 1 = 4$

   $a_2 = 3(2)^2 + 1 = 13$

   $a_3 = 3(3)^2 + 1 = 28$

Lesson 1.4

1. Each link in line 3 produces 3 copies, just as each link in line 2 produced 3 copies. So, line 3 will make 27 copies.

2.

Link	1	2	3	4	5
Copies made	3	9	27	81	243

   The sequence is 3, 9, 27, 81, 243,….

3. To find the next term, multiply the previous term by 3.

4. 3^L

5 a–b. Answers will vary.

Lesson 1.5

2. 528 3. 2850 4. 125,250 5. 720,600

6. 45 games

7. Yes; the first team will play 9 games. Not counting any games already counted, the second team will play 8 games, and the third team will play 7 games, and so on. I need to add the numbers $9 + 8 + 7 + 6 + 5 + 4 + 3 + 2 + 1$. I can use Gauss' formula with $n = 9$.

Lesson 1.6

2. 900 miles; 1500 miles

3. To find the number of miles traveled, multiply the speed of the car (in miles per hour) by the time driving (in hours).

4. 20 hours

5. To find the number of hours driving, divide the distance traveled (in miles) by the speed of the car (in miles per hour).

6.

Day	Time spent driving	Distance traveled
	hours	miles
Day 1	8	480
Day 2	10	600
Day 3	5	300
Day 4	7	420

7.

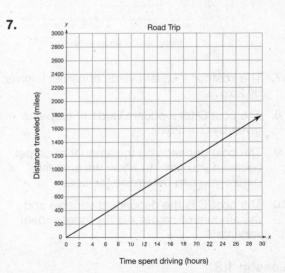

8. There is a pattern. The distance traveled increases by 60 miles with each additional hour spent driving.

Answers

9. The distance traveled for h hours is given by $60h$.

10. $550 = 60h$; 9 hours is not a solution of the equation because substituting 9 into the equation creates an untrue statement ($550 \neq 540$).

Lesson 1.7

2. The dependent variable is the distance d. The independent variable is the time t.

4. $416.67

5.

Amount of carpet (square yards)	8	11	15	22	25
Cost (dollars)	200	275	375	550	625

6.

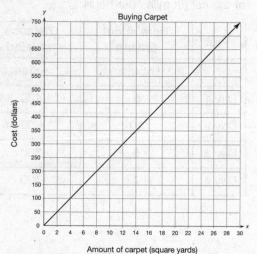

7. The cost for x square yards of carpet is given by $25x$.

8. The cost C for x square yards of carpet is given by $C = 25x$.

9. The cost depends on the amount of carpet because you have to know the amount before you can determine the cost.

10. The cost C is the dependent variable and the amount of carpet x is the independent variable.

Lesson 1.8

2. Total cost in dollars: $35(3) + 100 = 205$; It will cost $205 to store your furniture for 3 months.

3. Total cost in dollars: $0.25(200) + 30 = 80$; It will cost $80 to travel 200 miles.

4. Total cost in dollars: $0.25(364) + 30 = 121$; It will cost $121 to travel 364 miles.

5. Number of miles: $\dfrac{135.25 - 30}{0.25} = 421$

You traveled 421 miles.

6. The variable quantities are the number of miles traveled m and the total cost C in dollars.

7. The variable m is the independent variable and the variable C is the dependent variable.

8. The equation is $C = 0.25m + 30$, where C represents the total cost in dollars and m represents the number of miles traveled.

Lesson 1.9

2. The drama club sold approximately 50 candles.

3. The drama club sold approximately 140 candles.

4. The drama club sold approximately 450 candles.

5.

Number of candles sold (candles)	25	50	140	450
Amount raised (dollars)	150	200	380	1000

6. The equation is $R = 1.95c + 100$, where R represents the total amount raised in dollars and c represents the number of candles sold.

Lesson 1.10

2. Total cost for U R Connected: $40(60) = 2400$

Total cost for Push My Buttons: $35(60) + 100 = 2200$

3.

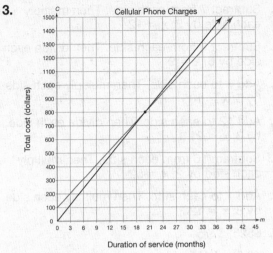

Cellular Phone Charges

4. The costs are the same when 20 months of service are purchased.

5. Push My Buttons is more expensive when fewer than 20 months are purchased.

6. U R Connected is more expensive when more than 20 months are purchased.

7. Sample Answer: The graphs are straight lines that start at the bottom left of the graph and move to the upper right of the graph. The graph for U R Connected is steeper than the graph for Push My Buttons. The graphs cross one another at (20, 800).

Chapter 2

Lesson 2.1

2. $\dfrac{3 \text{ marbles}}{12 \text{ marbles}}$, or 3 marbles : 12 marbles

3. $\dfrac{5 \text{ marbles}}{34 \text{ marbles}}$, or 5 marbles : 34 marbles

5. 6000 products

6. convenience sample; biased sample; 32 dentists

Lesson 2.2

2. cafeteria's recipe: $\dfrac{7 \text{ parts banana}}{12 \text{ total parts}}$,

Suzie's recipe: $\dfrac{4 \text{ parts banana}}{7 \text{ total parts}}$

Because $\frac{7}{12}$ is greater than $\frac{4}{7}$, the cafeteria's recipe has a stronger taste of banana.

4. 315 cups of banana

Lesson 2.3

2. $AB = 14$ cm   **3.** $NO = 12$ mm

5. 400 miles

6. $\dfrac{\$2.89}{1 \text{ gallon}}$; $72.25

Lesson 2.4

2. 40 children   **3.** 80 children

4. 150 children   **5.** 250 children

6. $5b = 4c$

$b = \dfrac{4}{5}c$

7. The number of children who brush twice a day depends on the number of children surveyed.

8. The variable c is the independent variable and the variable b is the dependent variable.

Lesson 2.5

2. about 41 female doctors

3. about 145 male doctors

4. $\dfrac{f}{m} = \dfrac{3}{7}$

$3m = 7f$

$m = \dfrac{7}{3}f$

5.

Labels	Female doctors	Male doctors
Units	doctors	doctors
Expressions	f	$\dfrac{7}{3}f$
	36	84
	60	140
	96	224
	117	273

Lesson 2.6

2. 6   **3.** 200   **4.** 300

6. $s = \dfrac{75}{100}r$

The variables show direct variation because $\frac{75}{100}$ is a constant ratio.

Lesson 2.7

2. You paid $29.75 for the sweater. This is 85% of the regular price.

3. The worker pays $222 in taxes.

4. Isabel's gross pay is $48,000 a year.

5. He answered 69 test questions correctly.

6. You should have 50 grams of protein a day.

7. Philip's heating bill went up by 30%.

8. You can incorrectly answer between 0 and 8 questions.

Chapter 3

Lesson 3.1

2. Subtract 11 from each side; $x = 15$

3. Add 7 to each side; $x = 38$

4. Divide each side by 4; $x = 9$

5. Multiply each side by 7; $x = 84$

6. Subtract 47 from each side; $x = 51$

7. Add 34 to each side; $x = 85$

8. Multiply each side by 9; $x = 76.5$

9. Divide each side by 3; $x = 187$

10. Subtract 74 from each side; $x = 144$

11. Carla will make $27.

12. $9h$

13. $9h = 108$; $h = 12$ hours

14. I divided each side by 9.

Lesson 3.2

2. Add 6 to each side. Then multiply each side by 4; $x = 24$

3. Subtract 3 from each side. Then divide each side by 5; $x = 7$

4. Add 8 to each side. Then divide each side by 4; $x = 8$

5. Subtract 7 from each side. Then multiply each side by 3; $x = 12$

6. Subtract 9 from each side. Then divide each side by 6; $x = 9$

7. Add 3 to each side. Then multiply each side by 5; $x = 105$

8. Add 12 to each side. Then divide each side by 3; $x = 21$

9. Subtract 16 from each side. Then multiply each side by 2; $x = 52$

10. Add 1 to each side. Then multiply each side by 6; $x = 120$

11. $525; $775

12. $12.5p + 150$

13. $12.5p + 150 = 1400$; Sonya can invite 100 people.

Lesson 3.3

2. 11 is 55% of 20.   **3.** 36 is 75% of 48.

4. 174 is 30% of 580.   **6.** $300

7. $E = 200 + 0.05t$; $3500

Lesson 3.4

2.

Labels	Fitness Place		Slim Chance	
	Time	**Total cost**	**Time**	**Total cost**
Units	months	dollars	months	dollars
Expressions	t	$40t + 75$	t	$30t + 150$
	0	75	0	150
	5	275	5	300
	15	675	15	600
	20	875	20	750

3. Fitness Place is the better deal for a 3-month membership; Slim Chance is the better deal for a 12-month membership.

4. Fitness Place: $c = 40t + 75$
Slim Chance: $c = 30t + 150$

5. a. 60 months   **b.** 36 months

6.

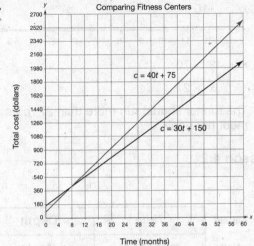

Comparing Fitness Centers

$c = 40t + 75$

$c = 30t + 150$

Total cost (dollars)

Time (months)

7. Answers should include: Fitness Place is cheaper for memberships less than 7.5 months. Slim Chance is cheaper for memberships more than 7.5 months. The two fitness centers cost the same ($375) for memberships that are 7.5 months.

Lesson 3.5

2. Clay is making a monthly payment of $80.80; Ethan is making a monthly payment of $110.20.

3. Joe: 456.27; Clay: 194.37; Ethan: 0; Only Ethan's account is paid off.

4. a. $b = 1485.27 - 85.75m$

    b. $b = 1163.97 - 80.80m$

    c. $b = 1320.4 - 110.2m$

5.

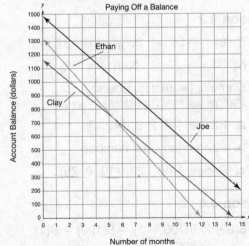

Paying Off a Balance

Ethan

Clay

Joe

Account Balance (dollars)

Number of months

6. Clay's balance is the lowest for about 5 months. His balance does not stay the lowest because Ethan is making a higher monthly payment, causing his balance to decrease at a faster rate.

Lesson 3.6

2. −13 is greater than −16.

4. −6   **5.** −3   **6.** 7

8. 8   **9.** 5   **10.** −6

12. 24   **13.** −6   **14.** 3

Lesson 3.7

2. $B(1, -2)$ **3.** $C(0, 2)$

4. $D(-2, 3)$ **5.** $E(-4, 0)$

7–11.

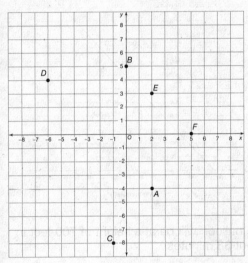

Lesson 3.8

2. The balloon will be at a height of 930 feet in 1 hour.

3. It will take the balloon 16 minutes to reach a height of 468 feet.

4. The balloon was at a height of 100 feet about 19 minutes ago.

5. You started your balloon ride about 29 minutes ago.

Answers

6.

Labels	Time	Height of balloon
Units	minutes	feet
Expressions	m	$10.5m + 300$
	−10	195
	0	300
	10	405
	30	615

7.

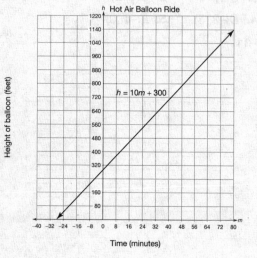

Hot Air Balloon Ride

$h = 10m + 300$

Height of balloon (feet)

Time (minutes)

8. The balloon will be at a height of 700 feet in about 38 minutes.

Chapter 4

Lesson 4.1

2. $4000 < x < 7500$

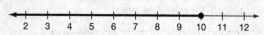

3. $x \leq 10$

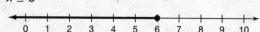

5. $x \leq 6$

6. $x > 8$

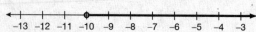

7. $x > -10$

8. $x + 43 > 70$

$x > 27$

The runner should run more than 27 miles to meet her goal.

Lesson 4.2

2.

Labels	Time	Depth
Units	seconds	feet
Expressions	x	$-102 + 3x$
	0	−102
	7	−81
	19	−45
	34	0

3. (0, −102), (7, −81), (19, −45), (34, 0)

4. Inputs: 0, 7, 19, 34; Outputs: −102, −81, −45, 0

6. The relation is a function. The domain is {−3, 0, 2, 4, 5}. The range is {2, 0, −1}

7. The relation is not a function because the input 4 has three outputs, 1, 2, and 3.

Lesson 4.3

2. $f(-8) = -56$ **3.** $g(-5) = 31$

4. $h(-4) = -27$ **5.** $f(1) = -2$

7. Domain: {all real numbers}, Range {all real numbers}

8. a. Range: {−4, 2, 8, 14, ...}

   b. Range: {any real number}

   c. Range: {−46, −28, −10, 8, 26}

Lesson 4.4

2. $8(99) = 8(100 - 1) = 8(100) = 8(1)$
$= 800 - 8 = 792$

Answers

3. $9(11 - 8) = 9(11) - 9(8) = 99 - 72 = 27$

4. $\dfrac{45 - 54}{9} = \dfrac{45}{9} - \dfrac{54}{9} = 5 - 6 = -1$

5. $\dfrac{26 + 16}{2} = \dfrac{26}{2} + \dfrac{16}{2} = 13 + 8 = 21$

6. $4(5x + 1) = 4(5x) + 4(1) = 20x + 4$

7. $\dfrac{15 - 6x}{3} = \dfrac{15}{3} - \dfrac{6x}{3} = 5 - 2x$

9. $6x - 9 = 3(2x) - 3(3) = 3(2x - 3)$

10. $5x + 35x = 5x(1) + 5x(7) = 5x(1 + 7)$
$\qquad\qquad = 5x(8) = 40x$

11. $16x - 40x = 8x(2) - 8x(5) = 8x(2 - 5)$
$\qquad\quad = 8x(-3) = -24x$

12. $8(9 + x)$ square feet; $8(9) + 8(x)$ square feet; When $x = 15$, the area of the rectangle is 192 square feet.

Lesson 4.5

2. -32 is an integer and rational number.

3. $\dfrac{5}{6}$ is a rational number.

4. π is an irrational number.

5. B **6.** D **7.** A **8.** C

9. $\qquad 5(2x + 3) = 3(9 + 6) - 27$
Given problem

$\qquad 10x + 15 = 27 + 18 - 27$
Distributive Property of Multiplication Over Addition

$\qquad 10x + 15 = 27 - 27 + 18$
Commutative Property of Addition

$\qquad 10x + 15 = 0 + 18$
Additive Inverse

$\qquad 10x + 15 = 18$
Additive Identity

$10x + 15 - 15 = 18 - 15$
Subtract 15 from each side.

$\qquad\qquad 10x = 3$
Subtract.

$\qquad \dfrac{10x}{10} = \dfrac{3}{10}$
Divide each side by 10.

$\qquad x = 0.3$
Reflexive Property of Equality

Lesson 4.6

2. $x = 1$ **3.** $x = 3$ **4.** $x = -2$

5. a. $11x - 200$ **b.** $9x - 50$

   c. After 75 hours the jobs will pay the same amount.

Lesson 4.7

2. 17 **3.** 32 **4.** 9

6. $x = -18$ or $x = 32$

7. $x = 5$ or $x = -\dfrac{17}{3}$

8. $x = 10$ or $x = 3$

10. $x < -2$ or $x > 7$

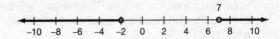

11. $x \le -10$ or $x \le 10$

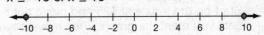

Chapter 5

Lesson 5.1

2. $y = 1.5x + 3$ **3.** \$13.50 **4.** 8 games

5.

Labels	Games	Total cost
Units	games	dollars
Expressions	x	$1.5x + 3$
	1	4.5
	3	7.5
	5	10.5
	10	18

6.

Variable quantity	Lower bound	Upper bound	Interval
Games	0	15	1
Total cost	0	30	2

Answers

6.

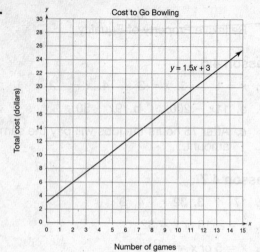

Cost to Go Bowling

$y = 1.5x + 3$

Number of games

7.

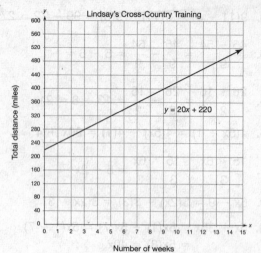

Lindsay's Cross-Country Training

$y = 20x + 220$

Number of weeks

7. The total cost of 12 games is approximately $21. Start on the *x*-axis at 12 and move up until you meet the graph. Then move left to the *y*-axis and read the total cost, which is about $21.

8. About 14 games can be played for $25. Start on the *y*-axis at $25 and move right until you meet the graph. Then move down to the *x*-axis and read the number of games, which is about 14.

Lesson 5.2

2. *x*-intercept: 5; *y*-intercept: –20

3. *x*-intercept: –3; *y*-intercept: –9

4. *x*-intercept: –4; *y*-intercept: –4

5. equation: $y = 56 - 7x$
x-intercept: 8; After 8 days, there were no pairs of shoes in stock.
y-intercept: 56; At the start of the sale, there were 56 pairs of shoes in stock.

Lesson 5.3

2. $\dfrac{540 \text{ miles}}{1 \text{ day}}$ **3.** $\dfrac{0.1 \text{ mile}}{1 \text{ minute}}, \dfrac{4.5 \text{ miles}}{45 \text{ minutes}}$

5. $m = -2$ **6.** $m = 0.5$ **7.** $m = -3$

Lesson 5.4

2. $y = -3x + 2$; slope = –3; *y*-intercept = 2

3. $y = 5x + 7$; slope = 5; *y*-intercept = 7

4. $y = x - 3$; slope = 1; *y*-intercept = –3

5. $y = 20x + 220$

6. slope = 20; *y*-intercept = 220

Lesson 5.5

2. $y = -2x - 12$ **3.** $y = \dfrac{1}{3}x + 4$

4. $y = 4x - 4$ **5.** $y = -\dfrac{3}{2}x - 2$

7. $y = -2x - 5$ **8.** $y = \dfrac{1}{2}x - 3$

9. $y = -\dfrac{3}{4}x + 6$ **10.** $y = 6x + 14$

Lesson 5.6

1.

Time since first bill	Debt
months	dollars
0	500
1	450
2	400
3	350
4	275
5	200
6	0
7	0
8	0

2.

Variable quantity	Lower bound	Upper bound	Interval
Time	0.0	7.5	0.5
Debt	0	600	40

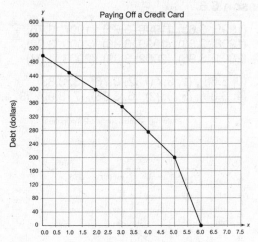

3. $y = -50x + 500$

4. $y = -75x + 575$

5. $y = 0$

6. First piece: {0, 1, 2, 3}; Second piece: {4, 5}; Third piece: {6, 7, 8}

7. $f(x) = \begin{cases} -50x + 500, & 0 \le x \le 3 \\ -75x + 575, & 3 < x \le 5 \\ 0, & 5 < x \end{cases}$

8. y-intercept: 500; The y-intercept represents Charlie's initial debt.

Lesson 5.7

2. $-3x + y = -12$ **3.** $x + 4y = 24$

4. $-x + 2y = -10$ **6.** $y = -3x - 12$

7. $y = -\dfrac{1}{4}x - 6$ **8.** $y = \dfrac{1}{3}x + \dfrac{7}{3}$

9. $4x + 5y$ **10.** $4x + 5y = 500$

11. The x-intercept, 125, represents the number of student tickets sold if no adult tickets are sold. The y-intercept, 100, represents the number of adult tickets sold if no student tickets are sold.

Lesson 5.8

2. $r = \dfrac{C}{2\pi}$ **3.** $t = \dfrac{D - d}{r}$

4. $n = \dfrac{S}{180} + 2$ **5.** $h = \dfrac{2A}{b_1 - b_2}$

Chapter 6

Lesson 6.1

1. (0, 20), (1, 21.2), (2, 23), (3, 23.5), (4, 25), (5, 26), (6, 28)

2–3.

Variable quantity	Lower bound	Upper bound	Interval
Years	0	15	1
Salary	0	45	3

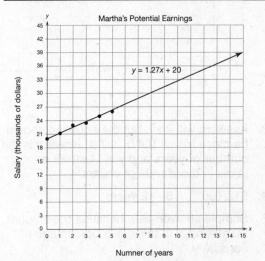

4. Answers will vary, but the equation should be close to $y = 1.27x + 20$, where x is the number of years and y is Martha's annual salary in thousands of dollars.

5. Sample answer: Martha's salary increased about $1270 dollars each year. The answer was given by the slope of the line in Question 4.

6. $32,700   **7.** $45,400

8. The answers seem reasonable, so my model seems accurate.

Lesson 6.2

1. (0, 7.4), (1, 7.844), (2, 8.51), (3, 8.695), (4, 9.25), (5, 9.6), (6, 10.36)

2–3.

Variable quantity	Lower bound	Upper bound	Interval
Years	0	15	1
Annual taxes	0	15	1

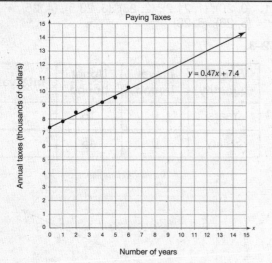

3. Answers will vary, but the equation should be close to $y = 0.47x + 7.4$, where x is the number of years and y is Martha's annual taxes in thousands of dollars.

4. $12,100   **5.** 12 years

6. Sample answer: Yes, because the amount Martha pays in taxes is a percentage of her salary.

7. The line representing Martha's annual salary is increasing at a faster rate because its line is steeper.

Lesson 6.3

1–11. Answers will vary.

Lesson 6.4

2. no correlation   **3.** negative correlation

5. positive correlation   **6.** negative correlation

7. no correlation

Lesson 6.5

3. 3.61   **4.** –11.7   **5.** $y = 3.61x - 11.7$

6. The value of r is about 0.98. This is a positive correlation because r is positive.

7. The data are close to being a straight line because the value of r is close to 1.

8. $y \approx 78.55$ **9.** $y \approx -47.8$

10. $x \approx 15.15$ **11.** $y \approx -1.75$

Lesson 6.6

1. (1995, 3.63), (1996, 3.71), (1997, 3.76), (1998, 3.83), (1999, 3.86), (2000, 3.92), (2001, 3.96), (2002, 3.99), (2003, 4.04)

2. (0, 3.63), (1, 3.71), (2, 3.76), (3, 3.83), (4, 3.86), (5, 3.92), (6, 3.96), (7, 3.99), (8, 4.04)

3.

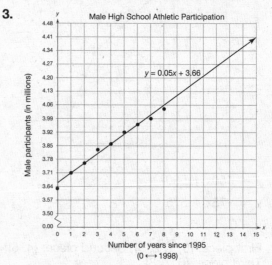

4. $y = 0.05x + 3.66$

5. The data are very close to forming a straight line because the r-value is approximately 0.99.

6. The slope is 0.05. Sample answer: The slope indicates the increase in the number of male participants for each increase in one year.

7. about 4.16 million participants in 2005

8. about 4.41 million participants in 2010

9. In 2011, there will be about 4.5 million participants.

10. In 1985, there were about 3.2 million participants.

Lesson 6.7

1.

Labels	Radius of circle	Area of circle
Units	cm	sq cm
Expressions	r	πr^2
	2	12.57
	4	50.27
	6	113.10
	8	201.06
	10	314.16

2. (2, 12.57), (4, 50.27), (6, 113.10), (8, 201.06), (10, 314.16)

3–4.

Variable quantity	Lower bound	Upper bound	Interval
Radius of circle	0	15	1
Area of circle	0	375	25

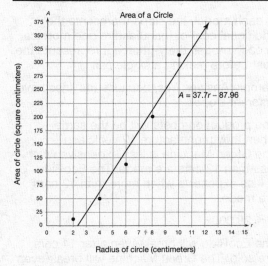

4. Answers will vary, but graph of line should be close to $y = 38x - 88$.

5. Sample answer: The data increases in a curve shape.

6. Using the area formula, the area of a circle with a radius of 20 cm is 1256.6 cm². Using the equation, the area is 666.04 cm². Because the data does not correlate well, the prediction is not accurate.

Chapter 7

Lesson 7.1

1.

Labels	Number of scarves	Product costs	Income
Units	scarves	dollars	dollars
Expressions	x	$y = 12x + 30$	$y = 15x$
	0	30	0
	5	90	75
	10	150	150
	15	210	225
	20	270	300

3. If Maggie sells 10 scarves, her profit is $0. If Maggie sells 20 scarves, her profit is $30.

4. The break-even point is 10 scarves because the profit is $0.

5.

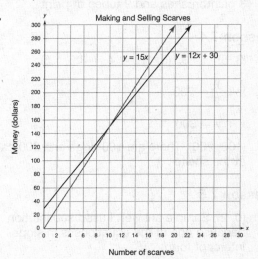

6. The production cost is greater than the income when less than 10 scarves are produced and sold.

7. The income is greater than the production cost when more than 10 scarves are produced and sold.

8. The income and production cost are equal when 10 scarves are produced and sold. This is the break-even point.

Lesson 7.2

2. The lines intersect at one point, so the system has one solution.

3. The lines have the same graph, so the system has an infinite number of solutions.

4. The lines are parallel, so the system has no solution.

6. The lines are parallel because the slopes are the same.

7. The lines are neither parallel nor perpendicular because the slopes are not equal and the product of the slopes is not -1.

8. The lines are perpendicular because the product of the slopes is -1.

Lesson 7.3

2. $(2, 8)$ **3.** $(-4, 3)$ **4.** $(-1.75, -2.1)$

5. $2.5x + 5.5y = 57$

$$y = 3x$$

The solution is $(3, 9)$. Cindy bought 3 paintbrushes and 9 tubes of paint.

Lesson 7.4

2. $(3, 5)$ **3.** $(0, 1)$ **4.** $(-0.5, 1.5)$

5. $x + \dfrac{y}{2} = 200$

$x + y = 300$

$(100, 200)$; There are 100 dogs and 200 cats at the shelter.

Lesson 7.5

2. $(0, 2)$; Sample answer: I used substitution because one of the equations is in slope-intercept form.

3. $(4, -6)$; Sample answer: I used linear combinations because both equations are in standard form.

4. $(-1, -7)$; Sample answer: I used linear combinations because both equations are in standard form.

5. $(-3, 8)$; Sample answer: I used substitution because the second equation can easily be solved for y.

Lesson 7.6

2. $y = 0.034x + 2.00$

3. In 2020 the supply will be 2.25 million registered nurses.

4. In 2013, the demand will be 2.442 million registered nurses.

5. In late 2014, the demand will be 2.5 million registered nurses.

6. In 1997, the supply was about 1.836 million registered nurses.

7. $-0.018x + y = 1.89$

$-0.034x + y = 2.00$

8. Sample answer: I used linear combinations to find the solution $(-6.875, 1.766)$. In early 1993, the supply and demand were equal.

9. There were 1.766 million registered nurses when the supply and demand were equal.

Lesson 7.7

1. Use x for the number of cars manufactured and use y for the total cost in dollars.

EcoRide: $y = 7500x + 275,000$

Green Machine: $y = 10,000x + 245,000$

2. In each model, the slope represents the additional cost of manufacture one more car. In each model, the y-intercept represents the cost before making a single car.

3. Sample Answer: Yes, because the lines have different slopes.

4. The production costs will be the same when they manufacture 12 vehicles. The Green Machine is less expensive when less than 12 cars are made. The EcoRide is less expensive when more than 12 cars are made.

5. $y = 28,000x$

6. The EcoRide will break-even after 14 cars are sold. The Green Machine will break-even after 14 cars are sold.

7. The manufacturers should not make the Green Machine because it is less expensive to manufacture if they make fewer than 12 vehicles, but it will not result in a positive profit until 14 vehicles are sold. So, they should make the EcoRide, but they should produce and sell more than 14 of them.

Lesson 7.8

2.

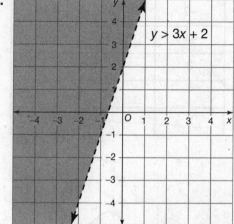

$y > 3x + 2$

3.

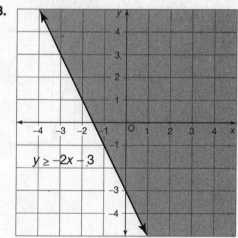

$y \geq -2x - 3$

Lesson 7.9

2.

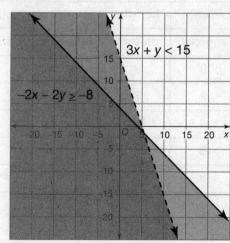

$3x + y < 15$

$-2x - 2y \geq -8$

3.

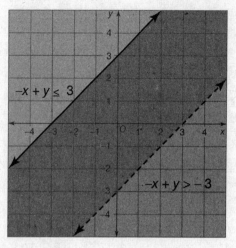

$-x + y \leq 3$

$-x + y > -3$

Chapter 8

Lesson 8.1

2. $a = -1, b = -4, c = 0$

3. $a = 1, b = 0, c = -8$

4. $a = 1, b = 9, c = -10$

5. $a = -\dfrac{1}{2}, b = 0, c = 20$

7. $g(3) = 23$ **8.** $g(-1) = 7$

9. $f(8) = 394$ **10.** $g(-2) = -31$

11.

x	$x^2 + 4x - 2$
−4	−2
−3	−5
−2	−6
−1	−5
0	−2
1	3
2	10

Answers

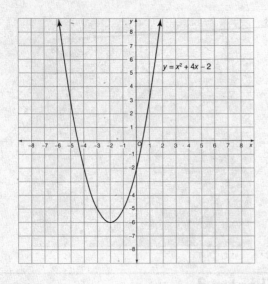

$y = x^2 + 4x - 2$

Lesson 8.2

2. (a)

x	$x^2 + 2x + 5$
−2	5
−1	4
0	5
1	8
2	13

(b)

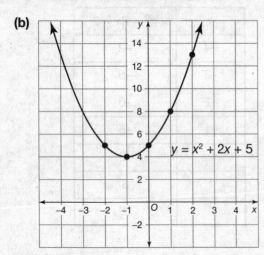

$y = x^2 + 2x + 5$

(c) $x = -1$

(d) (−1, 4); minimum

3. (a)

x	$2x^2 + x + 5$
−2	−5
−1	2
0	5
1	4
2	−1

(b)

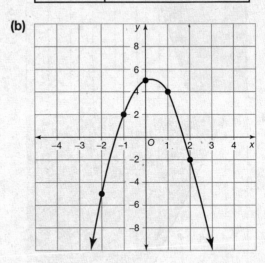

(c) $x = \dfrac{1}{4}$

(d) $\left(\dfrac{1}{4}, \dfrac{41}{8}\right)$; maximum

Lesson 8.3

1.

Width	Length	Area
meters	meters	square meters
0	9	0
2	7	14
4	5	20
6	3	18
8	1	8

2.

Variable quantity	Lower bound	Upper bound	Interval
Width	0	11	1
Length	0	11	1

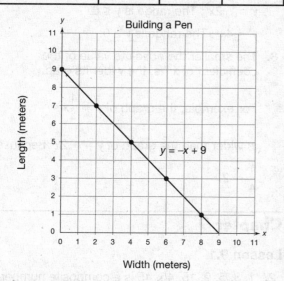

Building a Pen

$y = -x + 9$

Width (meters)

3. The function is linear because the graph is a straight line.

4.

Variable quantity	Lower bound	Upper bound	Interval
Width	0	15	1
Length	0	30	2

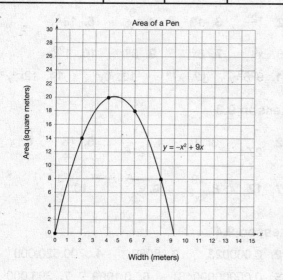

Area of a Pen

$y = -x^2 + 9x$

Width (meters)

5. The function is quadratic because the graph is a parabola.

6. The x-intercept is 9 and the y-intercept is 9. These values indicate lengths and widths that do not make sense in the problem situation.

7. The x-intercepts are 0 and 9 and the y-intercept is 0. These values indicate widths and areas that do not make sense in the problem situation.

8. The greatest possible area is 20.25 square meters. The width is 4.5 meters and the length is 4.5 meters. Sample answer: first find the maximum of the quadratic function to find the greatest area. Then find the x-value that corresponds to the maximum to get the width. Then divide the maximum area by the width to get the length.

Lesson 8.4

2. 1   **3.** 4   **4.** −12   **5.** −3   **6.** 11

7. −7   **9.** ≈ 4.8   **10.** ≈ 9.6   **11.** ≈ 8.2

12. ≈ 8.9   **13.** ≈ 6.4   **14.** ≈ 3.3

Lesson 8.5

2. x-intercepts: 1, −1; y-intercept: $-\dfrac{1}{4}$

3. x-intercepts: −3, −1; y-intercept: −3

4. x-intercepts: 3, 2; y-intercept: −30

6. $x = \pm 7$

7. $x = \pm 2.4$

8. $x = \pm 3$

Lesson 8.6

2. $x = -\dfrac{5}{2}, 1$

3. $x = \dfrac{7}{4}, -2$

4. $x = -\dfrac{8}{5}, -\dfrac{3}{2}$

6. The discriminant is positive, so the equation has two solutions.

7. The discriminant is zero, so the equation has one solution.

8. The discriminant is negative, so the equation has no solution.

Lesson 8.7

2. $0 = -16t^2 + 90t + 7$, $a = -16$, $b = 90$, $c = 7$

$$t = \frac{-90 \pm \sqrt{90^2 - 4(-16)(7)}}{2(-16)}$$

$$= \frac{-90 \pm \sqrt{8100 + 448}}{-32}$$

$$= \frac{-90 \pm \sqrt{8548}}{-32}$$

$$t = \frac{-90 \pm \sqrt{8549}}{-32} \approx -0.08$$

$$t = \frac{-90 \pm \sqrt{8549}}{-32} \approx 5.7$$

3. Sample answer: No, the negative solution does not make sense because t represents time and time is positive.

4. 133 feet

5. $a = -16$, $b = 90$

$$t = -\frac{b}{2a}$$

$$= -\frac{90}{2(-16)}$$

$$= 2.8125$$

The ball is at its highest point after 2.8125 seconds.

6. The ball reaches a height of 133.5632 feet.

7. The ball will reach a height of 115 feet at about 1.74 seconds and 3.89 seconds.

Lesson 8.8

2. If the coefficient of x^2 is negative, then the parabola opens down. If the coefficient of x^2 is positive, then the parabola opens up.

3. The vertex of all three graphs is (0, 0).

4. If the parabola opens down, then the function has a maximum value. If the parabola opens up, then the function has a minimum value. The minimum values of $y = \frac{1}{4}x^2$ and $y = 4x^2$ is 0. The maximum value of $y = -2x^2$ is 0.

5. The axis of symmetry of all three graphs is $x = 0$.

6. The domain of all three graphs is all real numbers.:

7. $y = \frac{1}{4}x^2$: The range is $y \geq 0$.

$y = -2x^2$: The range is $y \leq 0$.

$y = 4x^2$: The range is $y \geq 0$.

8. The smaller the absolute value of the coefficient of x^2 is, the wider its graph.

For example, the graph of $y = \frac{1}{4}x^2$

is wider than the graph of $y = -2x^2$ because

$\frac{1}{4} < 2$.

Chapter 9

Lesson 9.1

2. 1, 3, 5, 9, 15, 45; 45 is a composite number.

3. 1, 3, 9, 27, 81; 81 is a composite number.

4. 1, 61; 61 is a prime number.

6. $100 = 2^2 \cdot 5^2$ **7.** $245 = 5 \cdot 7^2$

8. $86 = 2 \cdot 43$ **10.** 3, 9

11. 3   **12.** no common factors

Lesson 9.2

2. 7^2 **3.** 13^1 **4.** $\dfrac{9^4}{4^4}$ **5.** 18^7

6. x^9 **7.** $8x^5$ **9.** 3^6 **10.** 1^{20}

11. $9^6 6^9$ **12.** x^{14} **13.** $6y^4$ **14.** $12x^3y^5$

Lesson 9.3

2. $\dfrac{1}{27}$ **3.** 1   **4.** $\dfrac{1}{216}$ **5.** 16   **6.** x

7. 12   **8.** $\dfrac{9}{x^4}$ **9.** $\dfrac{5}{3x^{16}}$ **10.** $\dfrac{1}{2}$

Lesson 9.4

2. 0.000023   **3.** 6080   **4.** 700,520,000

5. 0.00000090481   **6.** 0.1999   **7.** 393,000

9. 2.54×10^5 **10.** 6.7×10^{-4}

11. 1.508×10^{-3} **12.** 6.8×10^3

13. 4.22×10^{-4}, 4.71×10^{-4}, 3.995×10^{-3},

4.1×10^{-3}, 8.4×10^{-2}, 9.6×10^{-2}

Lesson 9.5

2. $\left(\dfrac{z^6}{z^9}\right)^{-2} = \dfrac{(z^6)^{-2}}{(z^9)^{-2}}$ Power of a quotient rule

$= \dfrac{z^{-12}}{z^{-18}}$ Power of a power rule

$= z^{-12-(-18)}$ Quotient rule of powers

$= z^6$ Simplify.

3. $\dfrac{(x^4)^3}{(x^4)^7} = \dfrac{x^{4 \cdot 3}}{x^{4 \cdot 7}}$ Power of a power rule

$= \dfrac{x^{12}}{x^{28}}$ Multiply.

$= \dfrac{1}{x^{16}}$ Quotient rule of powers

4. $\left(\dfrac{2x^2}{3yz^4}\right)^3 = \dfrac{(2x^2)^3}{(3yz^4)^3}$ Power of a quotient rule

$= \dfrac{2^3(x^2)^3}{3^3 y^3 (z^4)^3}$ Power of a product rule

$= \dfrac{8x^6}{27y^3 z^{12}}$ Power of a power rule

5. $\dfrac{6x^3 y^2}{3x^2 y} \cdot (5xy^3)^{-1}$

$= \dfrac{6x^3 y^2}{3x^2 y} \cdot 5^{-1} x^{-1} (y^3)^{-1}$ Power of a product rule

$= \dfrac{6x^3 y^2}{3x^2 y} \cdot 5^{-1} x^{-1} y^{-3}$ Power of a power rule

$= \dfrac{6x^3 y^2}{3 \cdot 5x^2 xyy^3}$ Multiply.

$= \dfrac{6x^3 y^2}{15x^3 y^4}$ Product rule of powers

$= \dfrac{6x^0}{15y^2}$ Quotient rule of powers

$= \dfrac{2}{5y^2}$ Simplify.

Lesson 9.6

2. $\sqrt[3]{-1000} = -10$ because $(-10)^3 = -1000$

3. $\sqrt[4]{625} = 5$ because $5^4 = 625$

5. $16^{3/2} = (\sqrt{16})^3 = 4^3 = 64$

6. $20^{2/5} = (\sqrt[5]{20})^2$

7. $x^{3/4} = (\sqrt[4]{x})^3$

9. $(\sqrt[5]{12})^3 = 12^{3/5}$

10. $(\sqrt{45})^2 = (45^{1/2})^2 = 45^{2/2} = 45$

11. $(\sqrt[4]{x})^{12} = (x^{1/4})^{12} = x^{12/4} = x^3$

Chapter 10

Lesson 10.1

2. terms: $5x^2$, $-x$, and 7; coefficients: 5, -1, and 7

3. terms: $2x^2$, $-3x^3$, and $6x$; coefficients: -3, 2, and 6

4. terms: $4x^2$, $-5x^3$, $-x^4$, and 5; coefficients: -1, -5, 4, and 5

Answers

6.

Polynomial	Degree	Classified by degree	Classified by number of terms
$16x$	1	linear	monomial
$3x^2 - 16$	2	quadratic	binomial
-9	0	constant	monomial
$-4x^3 + 7x^2 - 2x + 8$	3	cubic	polynomial
$-2x + 8$	1	linear	binomial

7. Graph the function. If you can pass a vertical line through any part of the graph of the equation and the line intersects the graph at most one time, then the equation is a function.

Lesson 10.2

2. $-5x^2 + 3x - 16$

3. $-2x^2 + 5x + 21$

4. $3x^2 + 4x$

5. $-4x^2 + 4x + 5$

7. $-x^2 - 2x + 9$

8. $7x^2 - 13$

9. $14x^2 + 9x - 2$

10. $-6x^3 - 2x^2 - 7x + 10$

Lesson 10.3

2. $x^2 - 81$

3. $-3x^3 - 24x^2$

4. $6x^2 + 25x + 14$

5. $5x^3 + 8x^2 - 17x + 12$

7. $x - 6$

8. $3x + 17 + \dfrac{104}{x - 6}$

9. $3x + 4$

10. $2x - 4 + \dfrac{32x - 62}{x^2 - 16}$

Lesson 10.4

2. $x^2 + 14x + 48$

3. $3x^2 - 28x + 9$

4. $4x^2 - 4x - 63$

5. $12x^2 + 7x - 10$

7. $9x^2 - 30x + 25$

8. $36x^2 - 16$

9. $9x^2 - 64y^2$

10. $4x^2 + 28xy + 49y^2$

Lesson 10.5

2. $-3x^2 + 9 = -3(x^2 - 3)$

3. $6x^4 - 15x^2 = 3x^2(2x^2 - 5)$

4. $8x^3 + 12x^2 - 6x = 2x(4x^2 + 6x - 3)$

5. $16x^3 + 24x^2 = 8x^2(2x + 3)$

7. $x^2 + 7x + 10 = (x + 5)(x + 2)$

8. $x^2 - 3x - 18 = (x - 6)(x + 3)$

9. $x^2 + 5x - 14 = (x - 2)(x + 7)$

10. $x^2 - 64 = (x + 8)(x - 8)$

12. $2x^2 + x - 15 = (2x - 5)(x + 3)$

13. $3x^2 - 20x - 7 = (3x + 1)(x - 7)$

Lesson 10.6

2. $\dfrac{x + 4}{x}, x \neq 5$

3. $\dfrac{2x}{x - 3}, x \neq -3$

5. $\dfrac{x}{3(x + 2)}, x \neq 0, -4$

6. $\dfrac{(x + 1)^2}{8}, x \neq 0, 5$

8. $\dfrac{6}{x + 6}, x \neq 3$

Answers

9. $\dfrac{(x-1)(x+3)}{3x(x+1)}, x \neq 7$

11. $\dfrac{21 + 10x}{18x}$

12. $\dfrac{5x-12}{4(x+4)}$

Chapter 11

Lesson 11.1

2. The probability is $\frac{1}{6}$ because there is 1 five on the cube and 6 total numbers on the cube. The odds are $\frac{1}{5}$ because 1 number is a five and the remaining numbers are not fives.

3. One person will win the prize, and 4 will not win the prize, so the odds of winning are $\frac{1}{4}$.

4. Because there are 4 girls out of 7 total contestants, the probability of choosing a girl is $\frac{4}{7}$. The odds of choosing a girl will be $\frac{4}{3}$ because 3 of the contestants are not girls.

Lesson 11.2

2. The experimental probability is $\frac{4}{10} = \frac{2}{5}$.

3. Theoretical probability is 10 times. Experimental probability answers will vary.

4. Theoretical probability is 1. Experimental probability answers will vary.

Lesson 11.3

2. "1" pieces of paper: $40\left(\dfrac{3}{5}\right) = 24$;

   "2" pieces of paper: $40\left(\dfrac{3}{10}\right) = 12$;

   "3" pieces of paper: $40\left(\dfrac{1}{10}\right) = 4$

Lesson 11.4

2. $\frac{3}{23}$

3. Region 4 is the largest region, because the spinner landed on this region the most number of times.

4. Region 3 is the smallest region, because the spinner landed on this region the fewest number of times.

Lesson 11.5

2. The interior designer has 40 ways to design the room.

3. There are 12 different options for the next picture that she will frame.

4. There are 16 different sandwiches that can be made.

Lesson 11.6

2. $_4P_3 = \dfrac{4!}{(4-3)!} = \dfrac{4 \cdot 3 \cdot 2 \cdot 1}{1} = 24$

3. $_{10}P_2 = \dfrac{10!}{(10-2)!}$

   $= \dfrac{10 \cdot 9 \cdot 8 \cdot 7 \cdot 6 \cdot 5 \cdot 4 \cdot 3 \cdot 2 \cdot 1}{8 \cdot 7 \cdot 6 \cdot 5 \cdot 4 \cdot 3 \cdot 2 \cdot 1}$

   $= 90$

4. $_6C_2 = \dfrac{6!}{(6-2)!2!}$

   $= \dfrac{6 \cdot 5 \cdot 4 \cdot 3 \cdot 2 \cdot 1}{(4 \cdot 3 \cdot 2 \cdot 1)(2 \cdot 1)} = 15$

5. $_7C_4 = \dfrac{7!}{(7-4)!4!}$

   $= \dfrac{7 \cdot 6 \cdot 5 \cdot 4 \cdot 3 \cdot 2 \cdot 1}{(3 \cdot 2 \cdot 1)(4 \cdot 3 \cdot 2 \cdot 1)} = 35$

6. $_5P_5 = \dfrac{5!}{(5-5)!}$

   $= \dfrac{5 \cdot 4 \cdot 3 \cdot 2 \cdot 1}{0!} = \dfrac{120}{1} = 120$

7. $_3C_3 = \dfrac{3!}{(3-3)!3!} = \dfrac{3 \cdot 2 \cdot 1}{(0!)(3 \cdot 2 \cdot 1)} = 1$

Lesson 11.7

2. $\dfrac{3}{100} \cdot \dfrac{1}{99} = \dfrac{1}{3300}$

3. $\dfrac{2}{100} \cdot \dfrac{1}{99} = \dfrac{1}{4950}$

4. The events are independent.

   $\dfrac{5}{100} \cdot \dfrac{10}{100} = \dfrac{1}{200}$

Answers

Lesson 11.8

2. The probability is $\frac{1}{6}$, because one triangle covers one sixth of the total area of the game board.

3. I would expect the number cube to land on the yellow surface 6 times, because $24\left(\frac{1}{4}\right) = 6$.

4. The probability of an event is the ratio of the number of favorable outcomes to the total number of outcomes. The geometric probability is the ratio of the area of the favorable region to the total area.

Lesson 11.9

2. Your friend can expect to hit the outer region 50 times, because $75\left(\frac{2}{3}\right) = 50$.

3. To score 300 points in three attempts, you would need to score 100 points in each attempt. The probability of scoring 100 points is $\frac{1}{3}$, so the probability of scoring 100 points 3 times in a row is $\left(\frac{1}{3}\right)\left(\frac{1}{3}\right)\left(\frac{1}{3}\right) = \frac{1}{27}$.

4. To score 150 points in two attempts, you would need to score 100 points in one attempt and 50 points in the other attempt. The probability of scoring 150 points is $\left(\frac{1}{3}\right)\left(\frac{2}{3}\right) = \frac{2}{9}$.

Chapter 12

Lesson 12.1

2. The most number of curl-ups is 52. The least number of curl ups is 17.

3. The distribution is skewed right.

4. The mean is about 32.3 curl-ups.

5. The median is 31 curl-ups.

6. The mode is 27 curl-ups.

7. The median is the better representation because the data are skewed to the right and the median is less than the mean.

Lesson 12.2

1.

School subject	Mean rating	Median rating
Mathematics	28.8	27.5
English	23.3	21.5
History	25.8	27.5
Gym	28.3	25
Art	33.8	37.5

2. The mean and median ratings for mathematics and English are close together.

3. Answers will vary.

Lesson 12.3

2.

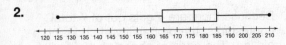

3. The outlier is 125; $Q_1 = 165$, $Q_2 = 178$, and $Q_3 = 190$

4. The interquartile range is 20.5. This is a large number, so the middle 50% of the data is spread apart.

Lesson 12.4

2. a. The mean is 31.

   b. 1: $31 - 31 = 0$

   2: $27 - 31 = -4$

   3: $20 - 31 = -11$

   4: $25 - 31 = -6$

   5. $42 - 31 = 11$

   6: $40 - 31 = 9$

   7: $34 - 31 = 3$

   8: $29 - 31 = -2$

   c. The variance is 388.

   d. The standard deviation is about 7.45.

Chapter 13

Lesson 13.1

2. $5^2 + b^2 = 8^2$

$25 + b^2 = 64$

$b^2 = 39$

$b = \sqrt{39} \approx 6.2$

So, the ladder reaches about 6.2 feet up the wall.

3. $2^2 + 3^2 = c^2$

$4 + 9 = c^2$

$13 = c^2$

$c = \sqrt{13} \approx 3.6$

So, the distance from Candace's new location back to home is about 3.6 miles.

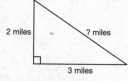

5. $10^2 + 24^2 \stackrel{?}{=} 26^2$

$100 + 576 \stackrel{?}{=} 676$

$676 = 676$

So, the triangle is a right triangle.

6. $1^2 + 2^2 \stackrel{?}{=} 9$

$1 + 4 \stackrel{?}{=} 9$

$5 \neq 9$

So, the triangle is not a right triangle.

Lesson 13.2

2. distance: $\sqrt{29}$; midpoint: $\left(\frac{3}{2}, 4\right)$

3. distance: $\sqrt{52}$; midpoint: $(-2, 3)$

4. distance: $\sqrt{148}$; midpoint: $(-6, -3)$

5. distance: $\sqrt{197}$; midpoint: $\left(-1, \frac{21}{2}\right)$

Lesson 13.3

2. $x \approx 10.69$; $x \approx 1.31$

3. $x \approx -2.615$; $x \approx -13.385$

4. $x \approx -2.836$; $x \approx -15.164$

5. $x \approx 0.923$; $x \approx -24.923$

Lesson 13.4

2. The vertex form of the equation is $y = (x - 4)^2 - 15$. The vertex is $(4, -15)$.

3. The vertex form of the equation is $y = (x - 6)^2 + 4$. The vertex is $(6, 4)$.

4. The y-intercept is 4. The x-intercepts is 2. The vertex is $(2, 0)$.

Lesson 13.5

2. The parent function is $y = x^2$. Translation 1 unit right

3. The parent function is $y = x^2$. Translation 7 units left

4. The parent function is $y = x^2$. Dilation (stretch by a factor of 2) and translation 3 units up

5. The parent function is $y = x^2$. Translation 5 units left, dilation (stretch by a factor of 3), and translation 2 units down.

Lesson 13.6

2.

Time since beginning of log phase (in hours)	Number of bacteria	Prime fractorization of bacteria
0	1	$(3)^0$
1	3	$(3)^1$
2	9	$(3)^2$
3	27	$(3)^3$
4	81	$(3)^4$
5	243	$(3)^5$

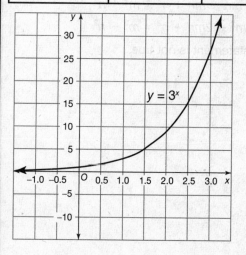

Answers

3. The y-intercept is 1. The y-intercept represents the number of bacteria at time 0 hours.

4. A function that represents the number of emails in terms of time since Monday is $y = 5^x$, where x is the time in days since Monday and y is the number of emails. Four days after Monday, there are 625 emails.

Lesson 13.7

2. $y = 150(1 + 0.02)^{20} \approx 222.89$;
The value of the coins after 20 years will be about $222.89.

3. $y = 250(1 + 0.10)^{50} \approx 29{,}347.71$;
The value of the baseball card after 50 years will be about $29,347.71.

4. $y = 13{,}500(1 - 0.25)^7 \approx 1802.03$;
The value of the car will be about $1802.03 after 7 years.

5. $y = 2000(1 - 0.30)^5 \approx 336.14$; The value of the computer is about $336.14 now.

Lesson 13.8

2. Answers will vary. Sample Answer: False. Some products can be purchased over the phone or by using the internet.

3. Answers will vary. Sample Answer: False. The quadrilateral could be a rectangle.

4. Answers will vary. Sample Answer: False. The number 10 is divisible by 2 but not divisible by 4.

6.
$$(m - n)^2 \overset{?}{=} m^2 - n^2$$
$$m^2 - mn - mn + n^2 \overset{?}{=} m^2 - n^2$$
$$m^2 - 2mn + n^2 \neq m^2 - n^2$$

The statement is not true.